MARRIAGE UNDER CONSTRUCTION

CONSTRUCTION

Let God Build Your Marriage

By

Harriett Nix

DEDICATION

This book is dedicated to my late, husband, Jackie Nix.

We built our marriage on these biblical principles.

With his humility, love, and commitment,

We had a wonderful marriage which became more

Beautiful as the years passed.

THANKS AND ACKNOWLEDGMENTS

I would love to thank the Lord and acknowledge His leadership, guidance, and encouragement through Scripture in the writing of this book.

I would like to thank my husband, Jackie Nix, for his hard work, as well as mine, in overcoming many problems and issues so that we could enjoy our marriage, which grew stronger and stronger over the years. Without his commitment to our marriage, this book would not exist.

I want to thank a few of our pastoral staff and some couples at Coggin Avenue Baptist Church in Brownwood, Texas, who read my earlier rough drafts and encouraged me. Also, I would like to give my thanks and appreciation to many friends and family members who encouraged and prayed for me as I conducted research to write this book.

I want to thank Rick and Yvonneke Beelby for serving as the models in the photo at the end of this book. Thank you to Kevin Smith for taking the photograph.

I want to thank Peggy Teague and Sandee Smith for their work in creating a cover design for the manual.

I want to thank my friends, Mary Vanderveer and Jan and Joe Stephens, for their help in earlier editing and encouraging me to continue writing.

I want to thank Jason Smith for his technical expertise in keeping my computer and printer up and running throughout this project.

Thanks to my nephew, Joshua Moore, who is an Architect in Rowlett, Texas, for his help with the knowledge of general steps in building a house.

Most of all, I would like to thank Sandee Smith for her hours and hours of editing, the cover layouts, encouragement, and advice during the time of preparing this book for publication. Without her words, work, and technical skills, this book would not have been completed.

MY JOURNEY IN WRITING THIS MANUAL

I would love to share the many adventures that were involved in writing this manual; however, that is almost a book in itself. So, I am only going to share the main highlights.

After my husband, Jackie, passed away, I felt extremely lonely. I went to a pastor friend and his wife and asked them to pray for me, and they did. Later that evening, I woke up during the night and realized God wanted me to write a book on marriage. I began to spend many hours collecting materials and ideas for the book. At times, I became discouraged and wanted to give up on the idea.

However, each time I started to quit, God gave me another encouraging Scripture. Habakkuk 2:2-3 led me to *RECORD THE VISION*. I read this several times, so I wrote down what I felt was God's vision, and it was then that I knew He wanted me to use the idea of comparing building a house with building a marriage. One day, when I really wanted to stop, I saw the words from Habakkuk 2:2: "*Record the vision ... THAT THE ONE WHO READS IT MAY RUN.*" With those words, I realized God had a plan, and I was obligated to finish the work the Lord had given me or be disobedient to Him.

The Lord used many other Scriptures to lead and to encourage me to continue laboring on, but these verses in Habakkuk 2 truly helped to shape and solidify God's desire for me to keep going on this journey.

It is my hope that each person who reads this book will run toward God, will run toward allowing biblical principles to guide their marriage, and will run toward a deeper, more beautiful lifetime commitment of building a strong foundation and great marriage.

Harriett Nix

MISSION STATEMENT AND PURPOSE

The purpose of this book is to encourage godly marriages by applying biblical principles, building strong Covenant foundations, and seeking to glorify God within the marital union.

Table of Contents

Introduction
Marriage Under Construction

Jesus is a firm foundation in our lives and in our marriages. A building implies solidarity, security, certainty, and permanence as opposed to frailty, insecurity, uncertainty, and transience.

In Ephesians 5:31, the Bible says, "A man shall leave his father and mother and shall be joined to his wife and the two shall become one flesh" (NASB). *Joined* expresses the idea of being glued or cemented together so closely that the union creates a oneness in which the couple has an intimate sweetness and togetherness that is permanent, like cemented bricks in a building. This marriage oneness should be a reflection or a picture of the oneness of Christ and the Church.

Steps in building this type of marriage union and oneness with a sturdy foundation are like the steps in building a house. Thus, "Unless the Lord builds the house [that is, the marriage], the builders labor in vain" (Psalm 127:1a, NIV). This book is intended to assist engaged couples, married couples, divorced couples, and widowed couples.

Many couples start a marriage on shaky foundations, or perhaps they start well but then stop the building process when problems arise. They do not know how to continue because their efforts are in vain. These efforts are in vain due to the lack of building their union on Christ and biblical principles. Utilizing biblical insights and applying them to their marriage creates a stronger foundation. God's word and His precepts, when applied to a marriage, develop an intimacy and a sacred love relationship that becomes strong, sturdy, and secure.

With this book, it is hoped that engaged couples and married couples who desire strong marriages can benefit by looking at the architectural steps in building a house, so they can see the similarities of scriptural principles in a step-by-step process of building a stronger marriage. To aid couples in this learning process, at the end of each chapter are questions to prompt healthy discussion.

In building a house, the architect draws up plans for a specific house with a specific purpose for the homeowner. In marriage, the architect is God, who has a purpose and specific plans for each couple in their marriage. God's plans have a firm foundation built on Jesus Christ, and He hopes couples will allow Him to guide their union into a permanent, cemented Christ-like oneness.

Land: Before Marriage

Psalm 127:1a tells us, "Unless the Lord builds the house, the builders labor in vain" (NIV). The land represents you. And before you build a house, you must prepare the land: clear away trees and shrubs, level the ground, among other things. Before marriage, your life should be cleared of all debris, rubbish, and baggage. Isaiah 57:14 says, "Build up, build up, prepare the way, remove every obstacle out of the way of My people" **(NASB).**

Consider these steps in preparing for marriage.

Get rid of excess baggage. Allow God to heal your heart of all past offenses, get rid of any critical spirit, and clear up the past.

- Get rid of anger, bitterness, and resentment. Clear your spirit. Seek a clean conscience. Pray it through. Pray until ALL hurts, anger, bitterness, and resentments are gone. List sins and iniquities. Pray over them. Forgive others and forgive yourself for past hurts. God removes even the guilt. Tell God "how much it hurts" … Then, move on.

Illustration: *The Sixteen Offenses*

A friend kept offending me almost every time we talked in person or on the phone. Many of the offenses she brought up were not true but were her assumptions about the situations. When I tried to defend myself or give an explanation, it made things worse. I was offended, heartbroken, and hurt! Finally, I got alone with the Lord and listed all sixteen offenses on paper. Then I talked to God, going through these offenses one by one. I told Him how much each one hurt me, and I said, "Lord, I forgive her for this offense. It hurts deeply; however, I forgive her." As I went through all sixteen, I cried and cried over my hurt, and through this process, God healed me totally. It was not a surface healing, but a deep spirit healing, and I learned how to deal with such things in a better way in the future.

- Forgiveness should be based on your commitment to forgive and not on your feelings. Feelings come and go— you forgive verbally, pray, and change your attitude, whether you feel like it or not.
- Ask God to help you clear up the past and get rid of past boyfriend or girlfriend hurts.
- Remove all past history—if not before, then during the marriage.

Illustration: *The Couple with Baggage*

An engaged couple planning to marry, who each had a lot of baggage, were given three choices by their counselor: 1) Get rid of the baggage together before their marriage; 2) Quit dating each other, work separately to clear their spirits and give up the baggage, and then start dating each other again; or 3) Get rid of the baggage early in their marriage.

Clean the slate. A clean slate, from both mates, helps build a better foundation.

Deal with a past marriage that has left feelings of rejection. Find your own identity and rebuild your own life as you address things like the following:

- Living with guilt
- Feelings of rejection
- Finding your strengths and weaknesses
- Improving or changing your weak points
- Rebuilding your past failures into your future assets
- Spending some time in prayer and fasting to face deep injuries that have been hurting for years; to have a clean slate, get rid of strongholds

Illustration: *An 80-Year-Old Lady*

In a Sunday school class of elderly women, the lesson was on forgiveness. The teacher mentioned that "a person should forgive someone even if he or she is deceased." Edith, an 80-year-old lady, was affected by that comment and stayed after class to talk to the teacher. When Edith was 14, her mother died, and her father remarried. Her father's new wife had two daughters. Her stepmother always mistreated Edith, no matter how hard Edith worked to please her. Over the years, Edith's hurt and anger built into a stronghold of bitterness toward her stepmother. Her stepmother had died years ago, and Edith, now 80 years of age, confessed to the Lord her anger and hatred toward her stepmother for her unjust mistreatment. Through prayer and confession, all of the years of anger, bitterness, and resentment left her. Edith's whole countenance was aglow, and she said to her teacher, "Oh, I feel like a great and heavy weight has been lifted off of me!" She was a new person, emotionally healed through the power of forgiveness.

- Forgiving others and asking for forgiveness, even if your past spouse is deceased

Be aware of the baggage. The baggage widows or widowers bring to a second marriage might be different. Baggage might be related to age, fears, differences between the first and second marriages, or the expectations each has for the second spouse. Both mates should spend time ironing out and getting rid of their own baggage.

- **Age.** If you are an older person, baggage may be seeing yourself with wrinkles or sagging flesh, so you may need to remove feelings of inferiority about age, as you will both have wrinkles and sagging skin. Strive to see each other as beautiful, because what truly matters is who you are on the inside.

- **Fears.** Perhaps you have a suitcase full of fears because you just buried someone who had cancer and now you are interested in marrying a person who has had cancer twice and is now in remission. 2 Timothy 1:7 states that "God has not given you a spirit of fear" (NKJV), and Proverbs 3:5-6 commands you to "Trust in the Lord with all your heart and do not lean on your own understanding. In all your ways acknowledge Him, and He will make your paths straight" (NASB). If God is leading you in this new marriage, commit yourself to Him and trust the Lord.

- **Differences.** Most likely, you will experience differences between your first and second marriages. Prior to your first marriage, perhaps you did not date much, or maybe you had a bad first marriage, or maybe fidelity issues occurred in the first marriage. Do not conclude that the second union will be the same. Pray about your love life and have confidence in God, even if you are older. Get rid of this baggage and look forward to a new and exciting relationship with your new spouse. Do not judge your new mate in the areas where your previous mate failed or had weaknesses. Remember, this is a new and unique person.

- **Expectations.** If you sense big differences in your expectations and the expectations of your new spouse, spend time communicating about your goals, desires, and mutual expectations.

Illustration: Don't Leave Anything Unresolved

On the day of my husband's funeral, before the services began, a lady came to me and confessed that she and her husband had had arguments that had not been resolved, and then he died suddenly. She regretted their lack of forgiving communication. All I could say to her was, "Ask God to forgive you now, and give it to the Lord."

Walk in agreement with your intended spouse. As you discuss your future together, come to a mutual bonding and understanding. "Can two walk together, unless they are agreed?" (Amos 3:3, NKJV).

Illustration: *"You are responsible for … I am responsible for…"*

Early in marriage, my husband and I came to a mutual agreement since we were older and had both lived so long as singles: He was responsible for the car, taxes, paying the bills, and yardwork outside. I was responsible for cleaning the house, cooking the meals, washing the dishes, doing the laundry, making the beds, and doing anything inside the house. It made me thankful to the Lord that my husband and I had left nothing unresolved.

Decide who will handle the checkbook, pay the bills, prepare income tax forms, and perform other similar tasks.

- Determine who will work and how much time that person will spend working.
- Establish who will take care of housework, yard work, automobile repairs and upkeep, and other similar tasks.
- Agree on how time will be spent with family.
- Discuss religion. If you have two denominational backgrounds, it is wise to agree on one or the other and go to church together.
- Consider goals and ambitions.
- Discuss having children.
- Talk about intimacy in the marriage.

The responsibilities of a household must be guided by priorities. For instance, usually the wife is responsible for keeping the house ("She watches over the activities of her household" Proverbs 31:27, NASB) unless both work and share responsibilities. The husband is usually responsible for keeping track of the finances for the family. A schedule can be created to assist with household organization.

Some women see no need for a schedule, as no one is looking or checking on them.

Illustration: *The Principals*

In teaching school, most teachers are totally responsible for their own lesson plans, classroom setup, curriculum, discipline, and control of the students. Most principals do not need to check on all those things, as they need to trust their teachers to do a good job. The principals might have to check on new teachers, but for the most part, they leave the teachers to do their jobs, knowing the teachers will be responsible.

When the man or woman operates on a "feel-like-doing-it" basis, sometimes it denotes unhappiness with his or her responsibilities.

Work falls into three categories. All work, whether drudgery, necessity, or fun, should be considered joyful when given to the Lord:

- Have to: Drudgery tasks = Tasks that drain energy and cause pressure
- Need to: Necessary tasks = Tasks are neither good nor bad, just needed
- Want to: Fun tasks = Tasks are creative and rewarding

"Whatever you do, work at it with all your heart, as working for the Lord" (Colossians 3:23a, NIV).

Answer the following questions.

(Answer only those related to your particular situation)

1. Engaged Couples and Married Couples:
   - Do I have any attitudes—anger, bitterness, resentments—I need to resolve?
   - Do I have any past history (boyfriend/girlfriend, past marriage/former spouse relationships, healed or ongoing hurts) I need to confess to God?
   - Do I have guilt over previous relationships? Do I need to forgive anyone? Is my conscience clear on all levels?
   - Am I aware of my past failures and weaknesses? Am I willing to let God change my failures? Am I willing to work on my weaknesses that need to change?

- Did we start off on the wrong path, and are we willing to make it right?

2. Widows and Widowers:
   - Am I fearful of having to handle tough situations again, such as nursing a new spouse through an illness, going through another bad marriage, or being fearful that it might get bad again with a new spouse?
   - Am I willing to trust God for the future with factors related to age (sagging/wrinkled/crepe skin, doctor appointments, or failing bodies)?
   - Do I see my new mate as a unique individual whom I can love forever?
   - Have we communicated our expectations and discussed them?
   - Am I willing to give up my home and the pensions of my deceased spouse and possibly have a lower socioeconomic lifestyle?
   - Am I willing to start over again and give up some of my treasured possessions from my previous marriage (furniture, larger living spaces)?

3. Walking in Agreement:
   - Have we decided amicably who is responsible for which areas?

- Are we in agreement on how to spend our money (checkbook, savings, or gifts to children on both sides)?
- Am I willing to accept my new spouse's family, flaws and all?

Architectural Plans: Eligible Mates

In building a house, the architect draws up and follows the plans. In Jeremiah 29:11, God says, "For I know the plans I have for you plans to prosper you ... plans to give you hope and a future (NIV).

Marriage takes planning, and it requires daily work.

Is it Well in Your Home? Some Thoughts by Billy Graham [adapted from a sermon]

1. God is preparing a mate for you.
2. Following God's plan, ask Him to show you the person He has prepared for you.
3. There must be love in the home—agape love.
4. There must be discipline in the home.

You must have Family Time in the home.

Consider these verses on the importance of planning and the benefit of working together:

- Jeremiah 29:11. "For I know the plans I have for you, … plans to prosper you and not to harm you, plans to give you hope and a future" (NIV). God knows the plans He has for us, so you and your spouse should also use planning to help build your marriage.

- Psalm 127:1a. "Unless the Lord builds the House, the builders labor in vain" (NIV). Marriage requires a total dependence upon the Lord to help two people build a strong marriage.

- Ecclesiastes 4:9-12. "Two are better than one, because they have a good return for their labor … A cord of three strands is not quickly broken" (NIV). God, the husband, and the wife form a threefold cord, which is not quickly broken.

In a person's choice of eligible mates, there are five basic reasons to marry.

1. Love – agape or lifetime commitment
2. Sexual attraction – friendship
3. Mutual complementary needs – likes and dislikes
4. Maturity or adult identification – responsible
5. Values – self-concept

In building a house, usually the architect makes plans for a new house, or a designer makes plans to rebuild an old house.

Illustration: *The Man and the Contractor*

A man told a contractor to build a large house and gave him an enormous amount of money. The man told the contractor to use it all. The contractor cut corners by using lower quality materials in order to make more profit. When the house was finished, the man said to the contractor, "This house is yours!" Not cutting corners means that you give your best, and you do not cheat. Plan for a lifetime of love.

(For more on biblical love, see I Corinthians 13, the "love chapter.")

A person who *wants* to marry has a better foundation for a successful marriage than the person who *needs* to be married to have needs met.

Illustration: *Learn to Love Others*

I went to my pastor and asked him to pray for a husband for me as I was getting older. He asked me why. He prayed for me— not for a husband but to "learn to love others." I was getting older and still single.

Love is a necessity when a person seeks to meet the emotional needs of his or her beloved. However, the emotionally needy person must seek his or her true identity in Christ and know that "God loves me!" Love is an unselfish devotion to the welfare of another. Philippians 2:3 says to "consider one another as more important than yourselves" (NASB).

The greatest emotional need of a woman is to be loved. The greatest emotional need of a man is to be respected. The person who is ready to be married is the person who can add stability to the marriage. The person who is ready to be married is going into the union with the idea of "What can I *give*?" rather than "What can I *get*?"

Answer the following questions.

1. Do I honestly believe I am marrying or have married the right person?
2. For married couples, do we have Family Time with each other and with our children? For engaged couples, are we planning to have Family Time together and with our future children?
3. Reviewing the five basic reasons to marry, what is the reason I married or plan to marry my spouse? Discuss each of these.
   - Love – agape or lifetime commitment
   - Sexual attraction – friendship
   - Mutual complementary needs – likes and dislikes
   - Maturity or adult identification – responsible
   - Values – self-concept

4. Am I starting a new life with my fiancé? Am I rebuilding the marriage I already have? What is my definition of love? What was or is my motive for marriage?

Quality Building Materials: Mate Selection Process

A builder selects quality building materials to produce a durable home. Discovering your motives for wanting a particular person directs the mate selection process. Sometimes people become involved long before they start thinking about this process.

The process also involves being willing to accept a person unconditionally, faults and all. However, if the person you plan to marry has a fault, has admitted that fault, and has asked for help or given you information so you can understand, then you can lovingly help by finding creative ways to "walk around the area that needs changing."

Illustration: *Martin and Mary*

Martin, a widower, told Mary, a widow, about being an uncommunicative person in his first marriage, which was not a fully happy marriage. So, Mary began, in the engagement stage, to lovingly remind Martin to be a good communicator. This got them off to a great start.

When change is needed, we should think of it as, "Change me, Lord."

- List ways God needs to change you. When you have listed and prayed for those changes, then obey and seek ways to creatively change. Evelyn Christenson's book, *Lord, Change Me* (2008), was written for women, but men can certainly benefit by reading it.

- Do not try to change your mate, but give your mate total respect and acceptance. Some people never change. Accept them unconditionally as they are because some changes are unimportant. If it is important, then do not plan to try to change the person before or after you marry. It will be a point of strife; it causes constant conflicts when you try to change another person. You cannot pressure people to be who they are not. Some people have such a strong desire to get married, but they see an area that needs changing in their future mate, and they think, "When we get married, I will help my spouse change." Usually, the woman is thinking this, but not always; however, this issue needs to be addressed before marriage.

Pray and ask God if the quality or trait you would like to see changed in the other person needs to be or should be changed. If God does not choose to change the person, then he or she needs to be accepted in love. If you feel strongly about the quality that needs to be changed, ask God if you need to confront the situation. If you do not feel at peace about confronting the situation, then do not do it. Instead, LISTEN to the Lord!

To help you discover your mate's love language, read *The 5 Love Languages: The Secret to Love That Lasts* (2015) by Gary Chapman. Your *love language* is whatever you do or say that tells your mate that you love him/her. This is a natural response. The five love languages are as follows:

1. Words of affirmation
2. Quality time
3. Physical touch
4. Acts of service
5. Giving gifts

Think through what you, as a couple, really believe. Do not assume that you know what your future intended believes. Discuss basic beliefs.

Illustration: *Four Months into Marriage*

My husband and I had been married for four months when we went to visit my mom and family. My brother invited my new husband to go fishing with him at 4:00 a.m. in the early morning. I did not know that anyone got up that early to fish ... it seemed like the fish would still be asleep! I was shocked by, and ill-prepared for, their adventure. Needless to say, this was new to me; however, later in marriage, we lived near the coast, went on many fishing expeditions, and had great fun!

"Know thyself." Know your own strengths and weaknesses.

Problem areas: Identify five problem areas and plan with your mate to solve them in a new and meaningful way.

Illustration: *Dirty Clothes*

After about four years of marriage, we discovered we had five problem areas that needed to be solved. One area was dirty clothes. Since my husband had been a bachelor for so long, he had a habit of throwing his clothes toward the hamper and the clothes not going into it. I spent a lot of time picking up clothes, putting them in a basket, and putting the basket in the closet. So, we worked together to solve one of our problem areas. My husband loved to do woodworking, and he had saws and all kinds of tools. I designed a wooden clothes hamper, and my husband made the wooden hamper with lots of design elements and a pegboard backing. Needless to say, he was so proud of his handiwork that he made sure his dirty clothes went into the hamper.

You cannot know a person totally before marriage. Just as house plans may need to be changed, you and your mate may discover issues along the way that require making changes. It takes a lifetime to know another person; however, after some couples are married for a long time, they may finish each other's sentences—

they know what their mate is thinking because they know each other so well.

Answer the following questions.

1. What is my motive for marrying?
2. Are there things about my future spouse that I am unwilling to accept or live with? (Refer to *Lord, Change Me* by Evelyn Christenson, 2008.)
3. Am I willing to accept my spouse or future spouse unconditionally?
4. What is my love language? What is my spouse's or future spouse's love language? Am I willing to build on our love language expressions in a manifested way, either audibly or visually? (Refer to *The 5 Love Languages* by Gary Chapman, 2015.) These are expressions of love:
   - WORDS – Words of endearment, encouragement, or praise
   - ACTS OF SERVICE – Gifts of service
   - GIFTS TO OTHERS – Expressing great worth by giving
   - TOUCH – Meaningful action that expresses love
   - QUALITY TIME – Spending one-on-one time with each other

5. Discuss your basic beliefs with each other.

6. For married couples, identify your marriage problem areas and discuss how you will go about solving them together. For engaged couples, list areas where you feel you might need help and discuss plans to solve them together.

Foundation: Principles, Commitment, Vows

A house built on a good foundation is sturdy, stable, strong, and secure. The same is true in a marriage: a couple should build their marriage on good foundational principles.

Illustration: *The House on Holiday Street*

When we bought a 1970s house on Holiday Street, everything was fine for a while, and no house repairs were needed. One day, though, after a rainy spring, followed by a hot, dry summer, the house began to shift on its foundation. Cracks developed, and as we were still under the foundation warranty, we called the company. The repairman told us the beam pipes under the ground were hollow and would need cement inside the pipes. Part of the house flooring was lifted, and the pipes were filled with cement and then lowered. After all of the work was done, our house on Holiday Street was level.

You have a 100% chance of a successful marriage if you do things God's way.

Marriage is a covenant, not a contract. A covenant is a sacrificial and permanent relationship. Consider these points as you think about marriage as a covenant:

- In a covenant relationship, you surrender your rights. You stay during tough times, during sickness, during tough financial times, and during troubled times.

- A contract is a signed agreement with one person holding up the agreement; whereas a covenant is between two people to uphold both sides and honor one another. In addition to holding up the agreement, we need to accept and work on our responsibilities. "For richer or poorer, in sickness and in health, and until death do us part," even when things get tough. In the covenant relationship, the husband has a duty to his wife, and the wife has a duty to her husband. "Desire is fire." Duty is work and commitment.

- We are loved by God, whether we feel like it or not. Billy Graham, in his devotional *Hope for Each Day*, says, "Feelings come and go, but true commitment stays" (p. 214, 2006). In a marriage, our commitment keeps us loyal to our mate.

- Marriage was created as a spiritual gift from God, and He has a plan for its success. He designed it so that a man and a woman can complete each other and become one in flesh, one in mind, and one in soul. Most people go into marriage with a 50–50 involvement of giving, but God's way is for each person to give 100%, regardless of what the other person gives.

- God has designed marriage with specific roles for each participant. The specific role of the husband is to provide leadership and to assume responsibilities for provisions, family direction, and love. The reason Adam was given a divine position as the husband was for him to be the head of the household.

- A successful marriage includes three elements.

  1. The first element is **love**—not just an emotional feeling or a physical attraction, but a deep commitment to put the other person first. This is an agape love or a godly unconditional love.

  2. The second element in a successful marriage is **maturity**. Too many are getting a divorce at the first sign of trouble. Maturity means a willingness to act responsibly and not take the easy way out. It involves a commitment to try and solve the problems.

  3. The third element, **faith**, must be present in order to have a successful marriage. With Christ at the center, a husband and wife praying and worshiping together strengthen their bonding.

- Love is a COMMITMENT OF THE WILL!

Doing things God's way means we must trust God and depend on Him. Proverbs 3:5-6 says, "Trust in the Lord with all your heart and do not lean on your own understanding. In all your ways acknowledge Him, and He will make your paths straight" (NASB).

As an individual and as a couple, we need to daily trust God for these four things:

1. Purpose
2. Acceptance
3. Identity
4. Security

Three Unchangeable Realities to Be Your Spouse's Helpmate

Unchangeable Reality #1: With God's help, you will find the right person for you—not a "perfect person," but the "perfect person for you." Colossians 3:12-14 instructs us on how we are to relate to each other:

"Therefore, as God's chosen people, holy and dearly loved, clothe yourselves with compassion, kindness, humility, gentleness and patience. Bear with each other and forgive one another if any of you has a grievance against someone. Forgive as the Lord forgave you. And over all these virtues put on love, which binds them all together in perfect unity." (NIV).

Remember, Christ is the only perfect person.

Unchangeable Reality #2: The reality is you must work at your marriage. Never say the word "divorce" or even think it; but you must say, "With God's help, we will …" This takes a lifetime of sacrifices and of yielding and submission.

Illustration: *Prayer*

As an engaged couple, my husband and I attended a marriage seminar. One of the suggestions for a strong union was to NEVER mention the word "divorce." So, the evening before we were married, as we checked to see if all was in order at the church, we decided to make a mutual decision. We got on our knees at the altar and prayed for God's presence to be real in our wedding ceremony, and we made a vow to God to never mention the word "divorce" to each other. We would seek God's help when things were tough. It was a great vow, and we kept it through 35 years of marriage. Not once did we even think of divorce. And God's presence was so real in the service that my unsaved nephew got saved at our wedding reception!

Divorce is a word that can become a weapon, and its use can cause major damage to your relationship. Ultimately, throwing the word "divorce" around can result in the death of your relationship.

Unchangeable Reality #3: Another reality is that God has a plan for your lives together. Satan, the thief, wants to "steal, kill, and destroy" your marriage (John 10:10, NASB). You must close the door to Satan and his tactics and accept and open the door to receive the abundance of God.

The Four Covenant Laws

The Four Covenant Laws keep unity in a marriage. Breaking any of these laws damages the marriage. Psalm 119:2 says, "Blessed are those who keep His testimonies, and seek Him with all their heart" (NASB). "All their heart" means complete commitment: your intellect, your volitions, and your emotions.

LAW 1 – The man and the woman *leave* their father and mother to become one with each other in a marriage. It is a picture of two people becoming one. Genesis 2:24 says, "For this reason a man shall leave his father and his mother, and be joined to his wife; and they shall become one flesh" (NASB).

Illustration: *Finances*

When they were newlyweds, I thought I should give my daughter and my new son-in-law some advice about how to handle their finances. My daughter's response was, "Mom, we got this!" It hurt me, but later, I realized they had left their fathers and mothers and were on their own from that day forward.

LAW 2 – The man and the woman *cleave* to each other. "What therefore God has joined together, let no man separate" (Mark 10:9, NASB1995). Cleave means to pursue with all your energy. Cleave also means to *glue* yourselves together with "super glue." You continue to pursue each other all your married life. You have to work on a marriage. All marriages require short-term and long-term work.

Illustration: *Glued Together*

Cleave means to glue yourselves together with "super glue." Consider this experiment: Glue two pieces of paper together, allow the glue to dry completely, and then try to separate the two pieces of paper. What might happen to the two pieces of paper?

LAW 3 – All decisions of significance must be made together. Husbands and wives share everything. Some decisions are minor and do not require the input of both; some decisions are major and should not be decided by only one spouse. Praying together allows the Holy Spirit to give you oneness in your decisions.

Illustration: *Major Decisions*

The pastor gave a sermon on the husband being the leader of the household and how a couple should be united in major decisions; however, if no decisions can be reached, the husband should make the final decisions. The pastor said minor decisions could be made by either the husband or the wife. An elderly couple

came to the pastor, and the husband bragged, saying, "We have
followed your sermon all our married life. I told my wife to make
all the minor decisions, and so far, we haven't had any major
decisions!"

LAW 4 – There must be purity in marriage. Purity is
conveyed in right attitudes and in right expressions. Attitudes and
expressions are revealed in facial expressions, 55%; in voice tone,
38%; and in words, 7% (Luna, 2020, para. 3). You must be careful
to be pure in your thoughts and your actions. After your
relationship with the Lord, your marriage should be the top priority
in your life. Ephesians 5:33 states, "However, each one of you also
must love his wife as he loves himself, and the wife must respect
her husband" (NIV).

Thoughts Related to Marriage from the Book of Nehemiah

Adapted from a Sermon by Matt Hagee (2024)

Nehemiah, a former cupbearer in the king's palace, came to
rebuild Jerusalem. He intended to do good works. We intend for
our marriages to have good works. Before building the project,
Nehemiah got permission as well as contracts as he planned the
project. If the parent is living, one should get permission, when
possible, to marry. No matter what the age, if the parents are still
alive, ask.

Illustration: *No Matter the Age*

My husband and I met when we were in our mid-30s, and when he asked me to marry him, I said, "Yes, but you will need to ask for my parents' permission." He did, and both parents approved of our marriage. Their approval was a precious symbol because we know they both gave their blessings.

If a spouse is deceased and children are involved, one should ask for the children's sanction and approval as well. This does not mean there will be no problems, but it may help to eliminate some issues. Some children, regardless of age, may have a difficult time accepting someone else as a step-parent. Do you wait until they approve, or do you continue with your plans? This will take lots of prayer, and each couple will need to decide what is best for how to handle the situation.

Illustration:

A widow wanted to date a widower, but his grown children were against it. She chased and dated him anyway. He did not want to remarry, as he said he had a bad marriage previously. The widow moved in with him, but when she got sick and went to the hospital, the widower left her.

Nehemiah continued to work even though there were problems.

When problems occur, evaluate the damage, personally and privately. Survey the problem by yourself. Work on the inside before you work on the outside, assess the needs, and solve the problem. Nehemiah worked alone to determine the issues. Do not involve others unless it is necessary, but survey God's design to guide you to a solution. Make sure you know God's way.

Illustration: *See a Problem*

Years ago, I worked at International Evangelism, a discipleship ministry. The founder and my boss, Billie Hanks, told his employees that when we encountered any problem, we were to think of three solutions and then choose the best solution among the three.

If you need help, work with those you know you can trust. Nehemiah only worked with his own trusted crew. Discover your goals together and know that walls are a source of protection. Gates control who comes in and who goes out. Take the bad stuff and kick it out. Walls in marriage represent allowing good people in, financial planning, emotional strength, and spiritual plans—practicing forgiveness and kindness—to create joy, peace, and trust in your marriage. Proverbs 24:3-4 says, "By wisdom a house is built, and through understanding it is established; through knowledge its rooms are filled with rare and beautiful treasures" (NIV).

Kick outsiders out. Nehemiah kicked out the enemies. "The God of heaven Himself will prosper us" (Nehemiah 2:20, NKJV). Do not let non-covenant people into your marriage. Leave father and mother and cling to your mate.

- Let go of grudges.
- Let go of wrong behaviors.
- Let go of problems and habits.
- Let go of bitterness.
- Let go of bad friends.

In marriage, we need to change from "I" and "ME" to "WE" in everything. I Corinthians 13:4-8 and 13 tell us, "Love is patient, love is kind. It does not envy, it does not boast, it is not proud. It does not dishonor others, it is not self-seeking, and it is not easily angered. It keeps no record of wrongs. Love does not delight in evil but rejoices with the truth. It always protects, always trusts, always hopes, and always perseveres. Love never fails. But where there are prophecies, they will cease; where there are tongues, they will be stilled; where there is knowledge, it will pass away. ... And now these three remain: faith, hope and love. But the greatest of these is love" (NIV).

Do not be a *debt collector* and do not keep a list of past sins. Get rid of the list of past sins and forgive your mate. To forgive does not mean you will automatically forget; however, we must apply Philippians 3:13-14: "Brothers and sisters, I do not consider myself yet to have taken hold of it. But one thing I do: Forgetting what is behind and straining toward what is ahead, I press on toward the goal to win the prize for which God has called me heavenward in Christ Jesus" (NIV). With God's help, soon the memory will fade, and you will have victory. Adopt an attitude of forgiveness and confess that you need God's help.

Another Biblical Illustration Related to Solving Marriage Problems

In building a house, sometimes the builder does not anticipate potential problems. Jehoshaphat, in the story from 2 Chronicles 20, shows us some principles that relate to solving problems. Here is an outlined list:

1. You must see the reality of the problem or conflict. Problems and offenses will come. No one can live completely free of offenses. You should accept your responsibilities instead of blaming others and defending your actions. Some people do not see the consequences of their sins or decisions, and thus, they do not take responsibility for their choices.

2. Two different people have two different backgrounds and different personalities, habits, and expectations. God has a purpose for these differences. Everyone is created with a

unique, one-of-a-kind personality. Add daily challenges and unexpected trials, and conflict brews. Daily challenges change with age.

3. Your initial reaction is usually "in the flesh," you can change your reaction to "in the spirit." Be respectful toward each other and give love and encouragement instead of criticism. Ask yourself, "What have I done to create this conflict?" Genesis 3:11-13 tells of a conflict in the Garden of Eden: And God said, "Who told you that you were naked? Have you eaten from the tree from which I commanded you not to eat?" The man said, "The woman whom You gave to be with me, she gave me some of the fruit of the tree, and I ate." Then the Lord God said to the woman, "What is this that you have done?" And the woman said, "The serpent deceived me, and I ate." Adam blamed Eve, and Eve blamed the serpent. Often, during conflicts, we try to blame others for our errors, shortcomings, and mistakes when we can (NASB1995). Paul tells us in 1 Corinthians 11:28, "Everyone ought to examine themselves before they eat of the bread and drink from the cup" (NIV). It is humbling to say, "Perhaps I am wrong. I usually am in our problems." (For more information, refer to *Automatic Influence: New Power for Change in Work and Life* (2016) by Erik Van Alstine.)

4. Recognize God's past help. Two possible outcomes from conflict are: (a) negative with separateness, and (b) positive with oneness and bonding.

5. Recognize your helplessness. Recognize the power of the enemy or the enormity of the problem and/or your own helplessness. A couple should have a plan for dealing with conflict, and it should include knowing, accepting, and adjusting to their differences.

6. Set your eyes on Jesus and receive knowledge of the answer from God, His presence, His leadership, and His voice. In John 15:5c, Jesus says, "For without Me you can do nothing" (NKJV). Next in resolving conflict and defeating selfishness is unconditional love, yielding our rights, humility, emptying ourselves, and giving to one another. We need to see ourselves as God sees us. Love is more important than problems.

7. Do not fear; the problem-solving will be clear. Pursue the other person with the intention of resolving the problem. Romans 12:6-8 says, "We have different gifts, according to the grace given to each of us. If your gift is … to encourage, then give encouragement; if it is giving, then give generously; if it is to lead, do it diligently; if it is to show mercy, do it cheerfully" (NIV). Sometimes resolving

conflict requires loving confrontation with an atmosphere of unconditional love and forgiveness. Ephesians 4:26 instructs us, "In your anger do not sin. Do not let the sun go down while you are still angry" (NIV). Remember their sins no more.

8. Listen for His direction and His timing. Resolving a conflict may require overlooking an insult. 1 Peter 3:8-9: "Finally, all of you, be like-minded, be sympathetic, love one another, be compassionate and humble. Do not repay evil with evil or insult with insult. On the contrary, repay evil with blessing, because to this you were called so that you may inherit a blessing" (NIV).

9. God rewards those who follow His directions and guidance. Blessings come when husband and wife trust each other, share intimacy, and pursue each other. Keep your relationship alive and vibrant.

Non-Covenant Relationships

Living together without being married or without making a marriage covenant promise is not a rewarded relationship. Living together outside a covenantal marriage relationship results in the following:

- You do not have God's blessings.
- You do not have God's favor.

- The truth is, you are living in sin.

- Sometimes, couples may experience a lack of trust after they marry.

- Sometimes, it leads to divorce later.

So how does a couple in this situation make their lives together a blessing? Are they doomed to failure and without the forgiveness of God? How can this situation be remedied?

- Turn to the Lord and ask for His forgiveness and genuinely repent.

- Change your direction as soon as possible.

- Either give up the wrong relationship or seek a legal covenant promise. Sometimes, it is too late for restoration. But if not, restore, reconcile, and clear up all issues.

Illustration: *Three Couples*

1. A couple is not married. He is saved, and she is not, but she is living with him because she is newly divorced and has no place to live. After salvation, she finds out the truth, but both of them refuse to make things right until five months later, because they desire to have a large wedding. This is not a good testimony.

2. A couple is living together to reduce expenses. Both are divorced and have children. They got entangled and are living in adultery. They are confronted by a pastor, and she moves out, angry. His response is godly, and he repents in front of the church.

3. An older couple is living together, but not married, because she would lose her deceased husband's Social Security pension. She still has her house, so she can have an address to receive the pension check. They are confronted by a pastor, but they refuse to make things right. The man dies one month later.

Again using Jeremiah …

Purpose in Marriage

What is your purpose as a couple? You have a call on your life as a couple in God's Kingdom. Everything is "little stories." The Big Story is God's purpose. Why did God bring you two together, and for what purpose, even if you started out on the wrong foot? God's Word tells us, "Faithful is He who calls you, and He also will bring it to pass" (1 Thessalonians 5:24, NASB1995). Jeremiah 29:11 tells us that God has great plans for us: "For I know the plans I have for you," declares the Lord, "plans to prosper you and not to harm you, plans to give you hope and a future" (NIV).

Marriage is an equal partnership. No one should be dominant, controlling, or demanding. The husband is the leader; however, he should lead in love and not in dominance. No one should be a bully or the one who forces things to be his or her way. This usually creates problems.

***Illustration:** Dominant Husband*

A man came from a family in which the father was dominant and always the leader. When this man married, he took on the same dominance in his family, like his father had. He was domineering in his marriage and with his family toward his wife and his children. When his children were grown and had left home, his wife left him, too. Imagine his surprise! She lived with another man and later married him. The divorced husband was so hurt and became angry, bitter, and resentful. He refused to date until he could find a wife who was "meek and submissive."

Both mates should have a part in talking about decisions, and there should be agreement on decisions. One mate should yield sometimes, and the other one should yield sometimes. In other words, there should be a compromise at times. Also, there should not be manipulation of the mate, but a genuine decision or compromise.

***Illustration:** Big Decisions*

When a married couple had to make major decisions, the wife thought of ways to convince her husband that her way was right. Then, she would use any method she could to manipulate him into following her plans and desires.

Share everything, even faults that need to be corrected. Do not be too proud to ask for prayer for help to remedy a shortcoming.

Spiritual elements in marriage are prayer and worship time together. Philippians 4:6 states, "Don't worry about anything; instead, pray about everything" (NLT).

Answer the following questions.

1. Have we followed the Four Covenant Laws for our marriage?

   - Law 1 – Leave father and mother and become one.
   - Law 2 – Cleave to each other; work on your marriage.
   - Law 3 – Make major decisions together.
   - Law 4 – Purity in our marriage.

2. Is there any need to confess or change our application of these laws?

3. Am I willing to follow biblical principles as in the examples of Nehemiah (Nehemiah 4 and 5:15) and Jehoshaphat (2 Chronicles 20)? If so, which story seems to match our needs?

4. Are there any problems or enemies in our marriage that need to be corrected?

5. For non-covenant (living together without being married) relationships (past or present), what needs to work or change?

- Am I willing to make a covenant with God and my spouse to get things corrected? A covenant is sacrificial and permanent. It is a lifetime promise!
- If I am living with my future spouse before marriage, how can I make reconciliation?
- Life-Time Commitment: Am I willing to *never* say the word "divorce" but to seek God's help with problems?
- What is our purpose in marriage? Do we have a call as a couple? (See Jeremiah 29:11-14.)

Building Principles: Concepts and Theories

In building a house, one must make sure the builder follows the plans and meets the owner's needs before starting the foundation work. A foundation is poured and dries, or cures, before the house is built. The pipes, drainage, and hidden work are included in the pouring. In marriage, laying a solid foundation paves the way for a more successful future.

Marriage mates should know each other before marriage. This does not mean you must live together unmarried, but it means you must spend time getting acquainted and learning the likes, dislikes, and ambitions of your soon-to-be lifetime mate.

Communication comes before and after marriage. You will discover that communication will increase after you are married.

Know thyself. Self-concept is to know who you are, to know what goals you have in life, and to have a good self-image and identity in Christ. *Who Am I? Identity in Christ* by Jerry Bridges (2012) is a good resource.

When a couple gets married, the principle is that each mate should leave their parents and cling to each other. Genesis 2:24 tells us, "For this reason a man shall leave his father and his mother, and be joined to his wife; and they shall become one flesh" (NASB). Are we following this principle, or are we too dependent upon our parents? Are problems caused by one spouse or mate being too dependent upon his or her family?

Set up some goals, directions, and core values for your marriage. This is like structural bearing walls and posts that are connected to the foundation when building a house.

- Set up some financial planning goals.
- Outline a few marriage role expectations for both you and your mate.
- These role expectations should not be based upon selfish wants and desires but upon God's standards from Scripture. These role expectations should also be designated responsibilities mutually decided and agreed upon by both mates.

Answer the following questions.

1. Do I have a good self-concept and a good self-image in Christ, or am I struggling with who I am? Are we both secure in Christ?

2. Do we have realistic expectations of each other? Do we see things we would like to change in our marriage or when we get married?

3. Previously mentioned in chapter 4, discuss the four basic needs in a person's life as related to their lives in general: (1) Need for Acceptance, (2) Need for Identity, (3) Need for Purpose, and (4) Need for Security.

4. Does either one of us need to let go of our parental dependence?

Change Orders: Understand and Accept Differences

Once the house plans are accepted, the architect, contractor, and builder come to an agreement and start building. However, if any changes need to be made, they should be made early so as not to hinder the building process. Early in a marriage, couples may need to make changes to strengthen their relationship.

Here are some examples of core values in the roles of the husband and the wife from Scripture:

- Be devoted to one another (Romans 12:10, NIV).
- Honor one another (Romans 12:10, NIV).
- Unconditionally accept one another (Romans 15:7, NIV).
- Practice unity with one another (Romans 15:5, NIV).
- Submit to one another (Ephesians 5:21, NIV).
- Serve one another (Galatians 5:13, NIV).
- Bear in love with one another (Ephesians 4:2, NIV).
- Encourage and build up one another (1 Thessalonians 5:11, NIV).

The core of marriage is to understand and accept your differences.

Illustration: *Exercise*

Because we are all built differently, when we exercise, some need to work on strengthening their legs, some need to work on tightening their tummy muscles, and some need to work on toning arm flab. But all people need to work on their core muscles for strength.

- We are not designed to live under stress.
- Four ways to accept your differences:
  - Complement each other's differences.
  - Celebrate your differences.
  - One mate should not dominate. If one person dominates, then there is no agreement. Husbands and wives should meet each other's needs. For instance, one week, pursue activities the husband enjoys, and the next week, pursue activities the wife enjoys. Alternate the choice of restaurants, whether you watch a football game or go to the symphony, whether you go camping or go to museums and antique stores for the weekend.
  - Sometimes in a marriage, people are attracted to someone who is opposite in personality and in character traits. This

does not always happen, but it is common that opposites in personality and character traits balance each other.

Illustration: *Quiet and Reserved, Outgoing and Verbal*

Usually, but not always, a person is attracted to someone who is opposite in personality. A newlywed husband was a quiet, reserved, analytical, thinking person, and he was married to a lady who was outgoing, social, witty, and verbal. They were a great blend for 45 years of marriage.

Focus on what you like about your mate. Focus on your blessings and accept your spouse as he or she is. Believe that God has given you the right person you need.

You need God's power and love to meet each other's needs. We usually meet our spouses' needs based on what we need. You must ask your spouse what he or she needs. Then, based on what your spouse says, you can meet his or her needs. Listen intently! Couples must be honest in expressing their real needs. Our needs provide a great opportunity for our obedience. In turn, our obedience provides the greatest opportunity for God's blessings and rewards. 1 John 4:18 tells us that "perfect love drives out fear" (NIV). Sometimes the person with past hurts has a stronghold of hidden hurts and is unwilling to express his or her feelings. Love and compassion expressed will help him or her to open up and share.

A couple needs God's love and power because they are usually opposites. Opposites attract; but in marriage, opposites can also repel. You need God's power to choose to forgive your mate. Marriage costs you something. Self-love destroys God's love. Part of love is to see each other's needs. Pray and ask God how you can meet your mate's needs in a godly way. If your need is not being met, turn to Jesus for strength and let Him provide for your needs or give you strength to endure until things change.

Illustration: *Mashed Potatoes*

One needs God's power to choose to forgive a person; with raw potatoes, you will need lots of muscle power to turn them into mashed potatoes.

Illustration: *Busyness*

A couple with children, where either one or both have a high-stress job, may tend to focus on themselves individually and not be open to expressing visible love to each other, as they are too busy.

This was discussed earlier, and it is worth mentioning again here. If the quality or trait you would like to see needs to be changed, pray and ask God about it. If God chooses not to change the quality or trait, then it needs to be accepted in love. If you feel strongly about the change, you may ask God if you need to confront the situation; however, if you do not feel at peace about confronting the situation, then drop it and realize the change may never happen (or you may change!). Allow God to do His work in your mate (and in you). In Ephesians 3:17b-21, Paul tells us, "And I pray that you, being rooted and established in love, may have power, together with all the Lord's holy people, to grasp how wide and long and high and deep is the love of Christ, and to know this love that surpasses knowledge—that you may be filled to the measure of all the fullness of God. Now to him who is able to do immeasurably more than all we ask or imagine, according to his power that is at work within us, to him be glory in the church and in Christ Jesus throughout all generations, for ever and ever! Amen" (NIV). Notice that the end of this verse says … "according to His power that is at work within us…"

Answer the following questions.

1. Together as a couple, write out your goals and directions. Look up the following Scriptures, find the core values in each one, and write these values out:

   - Romans 12:10
   - Romans 15:5 and 7
   - Ephesians 4:2
   - Ephesians 5:21
   - Galatians 5:13

- 1 Thessalonians 5:11

2. Which core values should we work on?

- Have I accepted my spouse and treasured our differences?
- What do I like and admire about my spouse or future spouse?
- Have I trusted God that I am married to the right person? If I am struggling, how can I eliminate the struggle and come to know that I am married to the right person?
- Do I honestly know the needs of my spouse or intended spouse? Am I willing to find out the needs and help meet them?
- Am I so occupied, busy, or working that I only have self-love? Do I continually express godly love with actions to my spouse?
- Is there an area, hidden or otherwise neglected, that we need to discuss? Are we willing to open up and have a compatible discussion? (See Ephesians 3:19-20.)

Building Preparation: Marriage Essentials and Prerequisites

When building a house, extreme attention must be given to the blueprints, for the basic layout of the architectural structure must suit the wants and needs of the owner. God outlines scriptural principles for marriage in the Bible.

The four basic needs in life (previously mentioned in Chapter 4, Foundation: Principles, Commitment, Vows) are the following:

1. **Acceptance.** God tells us in Hebrews 13:5b, "I will never leave you nor forsake you" (NKJV). You must offer total acceptance of an imperfect person for all time. That is what God offers us.

2. **Identity.** You should base your identity in Christ. Colossians 1:27 tells us that "God has chosen to make known … the glorious riches of this mystery, which is Christ in you, the hope of glory" (NIV). And Colossians 3:12 instructs us in how we should conduct ourselves because we are in Christ: "Therefore, as God's chosen people, holy and dearly loved, clothe yourselves with

compassion, kindness, humility, gentleness and patience" (NIV).

3. **Purpose.** You need a purpose in life. Your main purpose should be to serve the King. A good resource is the book *Who Am I? Identity in Christ*, by Jerry Bridges (2012). Another good resource is *Identity: 21 Days to the Real You*, by Peggy Teague (2020).

4. **Security.** You should be secure in your relationship with God and secure in your marriage.

These four needs are called the "Principle of Transference." If God does not meet these four needs, then we transfer that responsibility to people. People cannot meet these needs. We become bitter, cynical, and resentful because they cannot meet these needs.

Do not depend on each other to meet these needs. Depend on your relationship to Jesus. Jimmy Evans (2019) discusses practical, real-life challenges in his book, *Marriage on the Rock: The Comprehensive Guide to a Solid, Healthy and Lasting Marriage.*

Illustration: Walking on Water

When Peter walked on water, he failed the test and looked down, but he learned a lesson: Focus on Jesus and take His hand.

God has answers for our fears, our struggles, and our broken and hurt emotions. He will fix the problems or show you how to fix the problems.

Do not make your spouse be your "Jesus." Do not try to be your spouse's "Holy Spirit" or his or her "guardian angel."

Your most important relationship in marriage is with God. It is important to spend time with God and cultivate your relationship with Him.

God's view of mate acceptance is that the husband is head of the wife in leadership, and he is to love his wife, which is an action. The wife is to submit, adapt, and be in harmony with her husband and reverence him. The woman who will not accept her husband as he is cannot reverence him because reverence is an action. The husband and wife must submit to one another and esteem or think highly of each other. Ephesians 5:21 says, "Submit to one another out of reverence for Christ" (NIV). Philippians 2:3-5 instructs us, "Do nothing out of selfish ambition or vain conceit. Rather, in humility value others above yourselves, not looking to your own interests but each of you to the interests of the others. In your relationships with one another, have the same mindset as Christ Jesus" (NIV).

Myths about Marriage

Consider these myths about marriage. Do not believe them. If either of you falls for these myths, you will both be disappointed:

1. *"My mate will provide all my needs."* Not true. Your needs must be met by God: soul needs, spiritual needs, and other needs. It is true that the husband has the responsibility to provide for the family's financial needs; however, there are times when this cannot happen. For example, perhaps the husband has an illness or a disability. When you have a need for which your mate *can provide* and he or she does not know or understand your need, then you must share with him/her what you desire.

2. *"Sex is going to make our marriage great!"* No, what will make it great is intimacy and time spent with each other, including romantic moments. Sex will follow.

3. *"We will never argue, and we will be happy always."* No, when problems come, words are important. When you are wrong, say, "I am sorry" and "Please forgive me." When you are right, be quiet.

Illustration: *Fairy Tales*

A child, reading a beloved fairy tale, asks, "Mom, do you know how it ended?" Mom answered, "And they lived happily ever after." The child said, "No, they got married."

4.   *"We will be happy if we have this or that."* People are
     more important than things. The words "I love you" are
     important, so love one another with outward expressions.
     Love is an action; love is not love until it is expressed.
     More things will not make you happy. You will just want
     more and more. Two things are eternal: God's Word and
     people.

Before a house is built, the architect designs the basic layout
of the structure. A couple must prepare for the needs of their
marriage.

The couple has a purpose in the home. The husband should
have unconditional acceptance of his wife. She can be worthy, a
joy, and a crown, or she can be a destroyer. Consider these verses:

- Proverbs 12:4 – "A wife of noble character is her
  husband's crown, but a disgraceful wife is like decay in his
  bones" (NIV).
- Proverbs 31:23 – "Her husband is respected at the city
  gate, where he takes his seat among the elders of the land"
  (NIV).
- 1 Corinthians 11:7 – "A man ought not to cover his head,
  since he is the image and glory of God; but woman is the
  glory of man" (NIV).

The wife should be a wise builder, but she could be a foolish person and tear down her own household. Proverbs 14:1 provides a clear word on this: "The wise woman builds her house, but with her own hands the foolish one tears hers down" (NIV). The wife is a helpmate for her husband, giving love and respect. The husband is a protector and provider for the home. The wife has a responsibility of keeping the home in order, clean, and organized, taking care of clothes, food, and provisions, as has been mentioned previously. She sets the tone and attitude in the home. It should be a place of peace, excitement, encouragement, and love. Our homes reflect and affect who we are. What are we doing? Why are we doing it? How are we going to do things?

If you have something to say to your spouse, say it now. Do not wait until things fester. Proverbs 12:18-19 tells us, "The words of the reckless pierce like swords, but the tongue of the wise brings healing. Truthful lips endure forever, but a lying tongue lasts only a moment" (NIV). Pray first and make sure you are being led by God.

- If you have something to give, give it now.
- Be grateful now.
- Be content now.
- Do good deeds now.
- Share your riches now.

Interestingly, these three reasons for getting married are the same three reasons couples get a divorce:

- Sexual exclusivity
- Needs not being met
- Responsibility to take care of each other

You were created by the love of your parents. Psalm 127:3 says, "Children are a heritage from the Lord, offspring a reward from Him" (NIV). And you were created by God to love. You have a 100% chance of success if you do things God's way.

Answer the following questions.

1. Do I totally respect my spouse or future spouse? Have I given my spouse my total acceptance and unconditional love?
   - Romance – What are some creative ways we can improve our relationship? (For the unmarried: What are some creative ways we can be romantic but not have sex until we are married? How can we protect our future?)
2. Am I faithful to my spouse? What proves my faithfulness? If I have been unfaithful, have I truly repented to both God and my spouse with heartfelt sorrow?
3. Have we genuinely accepted our differences, and are we celebrating or complementing our differences?

4. The three reasons for getting married are the same reasons for getting a divorce: (1) Sexual exclusivity; (2) Needs not being met; and (3) Responsible to take care of each other. Are we weak in one or more of these areas? How can we solve these weaknesses?

5. Do we have some problem areas that stem from *Myths about Marriage* that we have accepted as real?

Preparation: Self-Esteem for Husbands and Wives

As the builder begins to put up walls for protection, a marriage must have inner protection. In the same way that the roof is covered, and the doors and windows are finished, a marriage needs protection.

You project onto others what you feel about yourself. You are favored, blessed, approved, accepted, loved, and valued by God. (See Ephesians 1:3-14.) Therefore, you should project your confidence in being loved and valued by God in your relationships with others, especially in the relationship you have with your spouse.

Put off your failures, your guilt, your shame, and your feelings of being condemned. Ask for and receive God's forgiveness. Look at who you are! That is your destiny as a child of God.

You cannot depend on emotions because emotions change so quickly. You need to learn to control your erratic emotions.

Love builds by action. 1 Corinthians 8:1 tells us that "love edifies" (NASB1995). Love expressed builds up another person. It builds his or her confidence, self-esteem, and self-worth. Love is not really love until it is expressed with actions. Christ expressed His love with the cross: "This is how God showed His love among us: He sent His one and only Son into the world that we might live through Him. This is love: not that we loved God, but that He loved us and sent His Son as an atoning sacrifice for our sins" (1 John 4:9-10, NIV).

Take the responsibility to build self-esteem in your mate. Philippians 2:3 says to "regard one another as more important than yourselves" (NASB1995).

Never talk about your spouse in a negative way. Always compliment him or her. Honor God and honor your spouse.

Invest in your mate and add to that investment. Work on your marriage.

You need an anointing to get married and keep an anointing to stay married.

Keep the battle attitude of FAITH that shouts, "My marriage will last!" Do not allow fear of a destroyed marriage to shake your faith. Before marriage, promise each other that you will never mention the word "divorce."

Be willing to be vulnerable and receive help when you and/or your spouse have problems. Young children want to be independent, and they do not want help because they want you to know, "We've got this!" So, a child will say, "I can do this all by myself! I don't need any help." Humble yourself to receive help when you need it.

Have a good attitude during times of problems and be faithful and joyful. You cannot have a healthy marriage until you have a healthy emotional attitude. "This is the day which the Lord has made; let us rejoice and be glad in it" (Psalm 118:24, NASB1995). Enjoy the journey!

Building Self-Esteem: Reject Feeling Unloved [adapted from a teaching by Beth Moore]

Feeling "unloved." If we feel unloved by anyone, we become vulnerable to attacks of the enemy.

Feeling "untouched" or "no hugs." We all need to be touched; for instance, we could all use a good back rub or a hug from time to time. All people need hugs.

Illustration: The Hug

I was single for many years, and a man at my church always hugged me when he saw me. His wife did not mind the side hug. It was the only hug I received each week.

Feeling "unprotected." We need to reject these feelings or find ways to know and understand God's protection.

Feeling a "lack of attention" or "inattention." We may lie or do something unethical to get the attention we want.

Feelings of "being criticized" or "opposed" in everything. We may experience these same negative or critical feelings toward others ourselves. We need to remember to please God and not man. Philippians 2:13 reminds us that "it is God who works in you both to will and to act in order to fulfill His good purpose" (NIV). John 5:30 reminds us that even Jesus said, "I can do nothing on my own initiative. ... I do not seek My own will, but the will of Him who sent Me" (NASB1995).

We may need to have our youth renewed. Psalm 103:1-5 says, "Bless the Lord, O my soul, and all that is within me, bless His holy name. Bless the Lord, O my soul, and forget none of His benefits; Who pardons all your iniquities, Who heals all your diseases; Who redeems your life from the pit, Who crowns you with lovingkindness and compassion; Who satisfies your years with good things, so that your youth is renewed like the eagle" (NASB1995). Yes, God renews our youth. Age is chronological, but youth is a state of mind.

Building Self-Esteem: The Root of Feelings of Rejection

The root of rejection. Matthew 12:33 states that "the tree is known by its fruit" (NASB1995). Rotten fruit equals rotten roots.

Illustration: *Roots*

Consider the roots of a tree or a plant. Think about the differences between a tree or plant with healthy roots and a tree or plant with unhealthy roots. Think about how the condition of the roots affects the fruit or flower.

The root determines the fruit. Everything comes from your roots. Do your roots need healing?

Illustration: *Feelings of Desertion*

When my husband and I had problems, I had inner feelings that he would leave me after an argument or a big disagreement. I went to counseling, and as we talked and talked about why I felt that way, we discovered some inner roots in my life that needed spiritual healing. My father and mother divorced when I was 12. I loved my father dearly, and because they never fought in front of their children, I did not understand the divorce.

Another wound, when I was 4 years old, occurred when my older sister died at age 7. My parents told me when I looked at her body in the casket that she was just sleeping. It created an emotional, deep fear in me when she did not awaken. As my counselor talked, I realized that because my parents had lied to me, it had created a stronghold of fear in me that someone I loved might leave me and not come back. I had never grieved over her death; so I cried and cried deeply, and I was healed in my inner being. I did not have that fear of someone leaving me anymore.

Burying or hiding things is not the way to deal with life. Deal with those buried or hidden things. Tell your future mate anything he or she might be able to find out later. Wounds from the past need to be cleansed. Hurting people hurt others. Bad attitudes need to be confessed and dealt with by God.

Get the knowledge that "God loves you." Separate the "who" from the "do." What you do or have done does not change the fact that God loves you; it does not change who you are. 1 John 3:1-2 reminds you that you are a dearly loved child of the King: "See what great love the Father has lavished on us, that we should be called children of God! And that is what we are!" (NIV).

You are not FREE until you no longer feel the need to impress people.

You cannot love someone else until you learn to love yourself. This does not mean that you are "in love" with yourself or what you look like, but it means you have accepted who you are in Christ, and you have confidence in your own talents, abilities, and capabilities. However, you should not have an attitude of arrogance or pride.

Illustration: *Arrogance and Pride*

A young girl was helping her grandmother arrange things when she moved into a new house. Her grandmother asked her to hang some craft beads on a stand. She suggested how to create a good interior design with the beads. The granddaughter responded with, "Oh, don't worry, Grandma, I am a great interior decorator!"

Sometimes, we come across as a prideful, arrogant, or haughty person who is unaware of his or her arrogance.

Building Self-Esteem: Possible Responses to Rejection

You avoid the risk of rejection by saying, "I will not try because I have been hurt."

You lack commitment when you say, "I will not make a paper marriage commitment because I was hurt. You cannot hurt me because I am not committed." Couples who live together without a marriage certificate usually do not maintain a long-term commitment, but they say, "Oh, we are just living together to see how it works out!" Ask them, "What is your reason for not getting married?"

Illustration: *Biblical Principles of Marriage*

A young couple was living together, and she had just gotten saved when I told her that, according to the Ten Commandments, she was living in adultery. She knew it was wrong and knew they needed to get married, but she gave all kinds of excuses. Finally, five or six months later, they got married because the church refused to baptize her as a new Christian until they followed biblical principles for marriage.

You conform to the environment just to get along with others, regardless of your personal opinions.

You become hostile and angry, so you reject the other person.

People who feel rejected sometimes have health issues or feel unloved. Satan may establish a stronghold in their minds.

Sometimes we get hurt and kid around, so we allow our past hurts and rejections to cause us to be sensitive to present events. Fear of rejection, as well as peer pressure, may cause us to be overly defensive and feel offended.

Building Self-Esteem: Overcoming Rejection

Base your life on what the Lord says about you and not on what other people say. A deep commitment to God is forever. God says, "I will never leave you nor forsake you. So we may boldly say: 'The Lord is my helper; I will not fear. What can man do to me?'" (Hebrews 13:5b-6, NKJV).

Pursue great Christian friends who will support you through thick and thin when you are struggling. Real friends are faithful and will tell you the truth. "A friend loves at all times, and a brother [or a sister] is born for a time of adversity" (Proverbs 17:17, NIV).

Expect rejection, but do not take it personally.

Forgive those who reject or criticize you. Treat them with kindness. (See Luke 6:2-31.)

When you are dealing with the issue of pain in your marriage, do the following:

- Let the past die and forgive yourself.
- Do not rehearse and relive things from the past. Forgive others, forget things, and move on. Follow Paul's example: "Brothers and sisters, I do not consider myself yet to have taken hold of it. But one thing I do: Forgetting what is behind and straining toward what is ahead. I press on toward the goal to win the prize for which God has called me heavenward in Christ Jesus." (Philippians 3:13-14, NIV). How do you forgive? And how do you forget being hurt? Forgetting comes with a renewed mind.
- Destroy the recordings in your mind of the past and let them go. You cannot relive and change a thing from the

past, so accept what you can and change the future. Let the past die and forgive yourself. Let it go.

A low self-image creates insecurity in the marriage. To marry quickly, the first person who asks, because there might not be another chance, or there might be no one else available, is a sign of insecurity. The insecurity caused by the fear of being left out could cause a person to seek the wrong mate.

Illustration: *Age 35*

In my late 20s, I dated, but it seemed the right person was just not on the scene for me. Finally, I met a nice young man and was ready to marry him, but for some reason, he dropped me flat one day, and he never asked me out again and never explained why he quit dating me. He never called again, and I was heartbroken. I started dating another man on the rebound, and we got engaged. But when he offered me a ring, I realized that he was not the right person for me. I developed a fear of never getting married because, by then, I was 35 years old. I had to turn things over to God in order to heal!

To create a higher self-image, you must change your attitudes of personality, character image, or self-esteem, which takes time. You must have a desire to change and the knowledge that you need to change. Go to the Scriptures and find your identity in Christ, and start working on believing who Christ says you are. Start with

Ephesians 1:4-14. This passage of Scripture contains a great list that speaks to who you are in Christ. You can also use self-image personality tests to identify your strengths and weaknesses, and to find your abilities, character traits, talents, hobbies, and other things you like to do in your leisure time. With God's help, you can accept the way God made you and love yourself as you are, but change things that need changing.

Answer the following questions.

1. What am I doing to build self-esteem in my spouse, as in Proverbs 22:1, "A good name is more desirable than great riches; to be esteemed is better than silver or gold" (NIV)? What steps do I need to take to build my own self-esteem?

2. Do either of us have some obvious feelings of being rejected or unloved because of wounds from the past or present that need to be dealt with? (Refer to the previous discussion on excess baggage.) Do I know the root causes of my feelings of rejection?

3. Walls in houses serve a useful purpose in that they separate the functions of each room. However, self-built walls in a marriage can separate our unity and our blessings. Am I responding to rejection and neglecting to build our marriage due to dysfunctional excuses?

4. What am I doing to express (outwardly or privately) my love actions to my spouse? Are we allowing our emotions to dominate our actions?

5. Are hugs and touches a part of our daily life?

6. Do we have some hurts, wounds, bad attitudes, or roots that need to be removed? If so, how will we deal with them? Do we need a deeper commitment to God so that we are willing to overcome rejection by taking the right steps with God for healing? What are these steps?

7. What are we doing in our marriage to support the anointing or the commitment that our marriage will last?

8. Do we need to get help with any of our problems? If so, who can we trust with our issues? Do we feel secure in our spouse's love?

9. Are we totally committed to each other with a lifelong marriage license and covenant?

10. Are there some scenes I tend to replay in my mind that I need to seek God in prayer to remove?

11. Together, do a Bible Study on Ephesians 1:4-14 and ask God to show each of you who you are in Christ.

12. Take a personality test to identify your strengths and weaknesses. (Various free personality tests and other resources can be found online.)

Painting and Installations: Working Together in Agreement

In building a house, the next step is to complete painting and installations. In preparation for marriage, some requirements must be met for things to work in agreement.

Consider the requirements in the following list:

1. Marriage requires that both spouses respect each other.
2. Each has a responsibility to endure the storms during tough times. Trying times are not the time to stop trying.
3. Marriage must be fun. Romance must be cultivated, and each spouse must find the fun level of his or her mate.
4. Resolve to prove your faithfulness. Figure out ways to let your spouse know that you are faithful so he or she can be comforted in your loyalty. Romans 6:12 tells us, "Therefore do not let sin reign in your mortal body so that you obey its evil desires" (NIV). Guard your eyes!

5. Marriage requires focus. It is not what you "think, feel, or want," but what you know about God that is important: "I know my redeemer lives" (Job 19:25a, NIV).

6. Pray that God will close doors that cannot be closed and open doors that cannot be opened until you both are in His perfect will.

7. A wife is a helpmate, her husband's "divine help," his Ebenezer (see 1 Samuel 7:12). But she is not his Holy Spirit! We cannot say this enough.

8. Speak sweet words to one another.

9. Speak soft and tender words to one another.

10. Speak sensitive words to one another.

11. Speak strengthening words to one another.

12. Speak kind words to one another. Remember, "Anxiety weighs down the heart, but a kind word cheers it up" (Proverbs 12:25, NIV).

13. Speak blessings over one another. Receive a blessing and touch your mate as you pass by.

14. Speak words of truth to one another.

15. In your relationship with your spouse, all issues give God an opportunity to teach you both, so communication is the best route to learning and understanding.

16. A husband should never compare his wife's body to another woman's body. Meet the sexual needs of your spouse.

Illustration: *The Old Photograph*

Over the years, the wife had gotten extremely overweight. The husband, due to good metabolism, could eat all he wanted and remain slender. As they grew older, he would take out a photograph of her when she was younger and thinner, and he would show it to everyone and say, "This is who I married."

17. Never refer to your mate as "old lady" or "old man." Never say things like, "My husband/wife knows he or she has to say good things about me, or I will slap him or her." Completely rid your relationship of these loveless expressions.

Answer the following questions.

1. Am I accepting my responsibilities as a wife? Am I accepting my responsibilities as a husband?

2. Are my words sweet, soft and tender, sensitive, strengthening, kind, truthful, and blessing words? Am I harsh, cruel, loud, unkind, deceiving, and dominating with

my words? Is my body language saying something different than my words?

3. What are we doing as a couple to have fun and cultivate our romantic life?

4. Am I accepting my spouse's personality exactly as he or she is, warts and all?

Differences in the Plan: What Makes Us Unique?

Just as a builder designs unique kitchen and bathroom cabinets, countertops, and sinks to suit the owner, so there are unique differences in marriage mates.

All couples have different strengths and weaknesses.

Illustration: *Painting Cabinets*

We moved into a 1970s house, and the cabinets in the kitchen were old and brown, so I wanted to paint them ... 15 cabinets! My husband dreaded the job as he was not a painter. We also had two large sheds in a small backyard. I wanted to get rid of the sheds and just have a yard to enjoy. My husband saw lots of good storage, and he wanted to keep them. We had some good disagreements about the sheds and the cabinets, so finally, I said to him, "I have found someone to come and get both sheds and take them down and remove them; so if you let me get rid of them, I will never ask you to paint these 15 cabinets again." When he said, "Yes," we made an agreement compromise. We got rid of the sheds, and I never mentioned painting the cabinets again. I just lived with the brown cabinets and put new hinges and handles on them.

Sometimes, couples with strong differences become angry when there is no compromise. One mate gets bitter, and a root of bitterness grows when the anger builds up.

Domineering attitude or dominance of one mate. In some marriages, one person is domineering or dominant and the other is quiet, not a people person, and very easy to please. The shy or quiet person does not want to make any decisions as he or she either has no preference or does not enjoy making decisions. The domineering person should not be arrogant nor prideful and should not consider or feel he or she is more important nor should he or she make all of the decisions.

Illustration: *Domineering Husband*

A young girl married at the age of 17, and she did not know she had married an extremely domineering man. They stayed together until the children were grown, and then they divorced. She had days of depression all through their marriage, but when they divorced, she was depressed all the rest of her life. She became a recluse and never fully recovered from that deep depression.

Sometimes one or the other of these personalities becomes "indifferent," and the couple slowly drifts apart.

The strengths of each mate will help complement your marriage.

Understand your own strengths and differences. Understanding your mate's strengths will bless your marriage. You will have a stronger marriage when these strengths are encouraged and recognized as assets and not liabilities.

Do not focus on the weaknesses of your mate. This is a destructive factor; instead, focus on the strengths. Three tactics in a marriage will help: (1) deny yourself; (2) do not accuse your mate; and (3) do not attack your mate.

Figure out your own strengths. Some strengths include the following (there are many more):

- Empathy – Feelings and thoughts of understanding and having sensitivity to others' needs
- Self-assurance – Confidence in oneself and in one's abilities
- Command – The ability to make good decisions; not domineering; includes others in decision making
- Belief – Having faith even when things go wrong or seem to have no answer

- Achiever – A person who desires to accomplish a high degree and quality of work or produce much work
- Relator – A person who is task-oriented and relational, and sees good in people or sees good in bad situations
- Learner – A person who loves to learn and share learned materials
- Developer – A person who loves to develop ideas and is creative
- Activator – A person who has a captivating personality and can help make things happen

Instead of complaining, here are some suggestions for complementing your differences:

- Pray for a vision or idea on how to solve the problem.
- Do not complain unless you are willing to solve the problem.
- Focus on the blessings rather than on the problems.
- Be grateful and thankful for things that create joy instead of complaining.

Illustration: *Thankfulness Booklet or Journal*

A couple could create a booklet or journal to write things for which they are thankful to the Lord for His provision. They could add photos of things they are grateful for, such as pictures of their family, their home, leisure activities, and time spent together.

Answer the following questions.

1. Each spouse should create their own list of strengths. Work on your strengths. As a couple, if you discover quickly that you have a huge gap in your personalities, perhaps you may want to write a letter to each other recognizing the differences and expressing your love and trust to accept each other fully in these differences.

2. Am I expressing gratefulness, or am I complaining? Am I being negative or critical of my spouse in front of others? Perhaps you might want to work on a "Thankfulness Journal" together, thanking God for your and your spouse's strengths.

3. What qualities do I most admire in my spouse? Do I express my appreciation, admiration, and approval of these? Spend time picturing the potential in your spouse. Share with your spouse what you feel is their future potential and bless them with a commitment to help them reach their full potential.

4. What are our mutual interests? Am I willing to share my spouse's interests (hunting, fishing, golfing, shopping, photography, cooking, woodworking, etc.) even if I do not have the same interests as my spouse?

5. When you deal with the problem of "your way" or "my way," how willing are you to let go and do it your spouse's way? Together, you can pray for a vision or an idea on how to solve your problem.

6. Am I honestly a supportive spouse? List ways to support your spouse. List people who support you as a couple. Pray for them and spend time fellowshipping with your best support friends.

7. How am I investing or working on my marriage? In other words, am I focusing on our blessings, or focusing on our problems?

8. What makes my mate unique to me? Do I appreciate that uniqueness?

Hidden Things: Build Inside

All houses must have pipes, drainage systems, and electrical wires to function properly. In a marriage, certain things must constantly function correctly, or the marriage will not have stability.

If God will "supply all my needs" (Philippians 4:19, NASB1995), why should I seek to find my mate's needs? Consider these verses:

- Galatians 5:13 – "You, my brothers and sisters, were called to be free. But do not use your freedom to indulge the flesh; rather, serve one another humbly in love" (NIV).

- Matthew 20:28 – "… the Son of Man did not come to be served, but to serve, and to give his life as a ransom for many" (NIV).

- John 13:14-15 – "Now that I, your Lord and Teacher, have washed your feet, you also should wash one another's feet. I have set you an example that you should do as I have done for you" (NIV).

The Husband's Needs

Consider these questions:

1. Does he spend time with God? Does he have an excitement for God?
2. Is he enchanted with his wife?
3. Does he speak tenderly to her and about her?
4. Does he share his life with her? In other words, is he open and honest?
5. Does he share his business and his environment with her?
6. Does he express either verbally or in actions his love for her?
7. Does he desire to communicate details with his wife about his life?
8. Does he have a special voice and love words for her? For example, does he have a pet name or a loving name for her?
9. Is there unity and oneness with his wife and with Christ (John 17:22, "I have given them the glory that you gave me, that they may be one as we are one," NIV)? In your daily devotional, pray specific things for your husband. The wife might make a list of her husband's assets and thank God for his strengths.

Expected investment in marriage is intense (Deuteronomy 30:19, "This day I call the heavens and the earth as witnesses against you that I have set before you life and death, blessings and curses. Now choose life, so that you and your children may live," NIV). God has given us a choice: Choose life or choose death. Your choices make a difference in your life, in your children's lives, and in your grandchildren's lives. A blessing is not a blessing until it is spoken or acted upon. The husband may need the wife to say how proud she is of him. Others can express how proud they are of him, but the husband is like a cork on water; the cork needs water to float. The wife is the water. Express things you are proud of and praise him. Do not complain, but honor him.

A basic need of the man is admiration and approval. Do not address his faults, but praise and compliment his good qualities. Barriers can be awkwardness, no qualities to admire, no conditions for change, and failure to accept him at face value unconditionally.

- Proverbs 31:10 – "A wife of noble character who can find? She is worth far more than rubies" (NIV).
- Philippians 2:13 – "… for it is God who works in you to will and to act in order to fulfill his good purpose" (NIV).

Respect and honor your husband. To honor him is to let him make mistakes or to do wrong. Do not lecture or browbeat him because of his weakness. He is head of the household, and he is responsible for his actions. Some men will learn from their mistakes or wrongdoing. For others, it will take some time before they learn. (Ephesians 5:33, "However, each one of you also must love his wife as he loves himself, and the wife must respect her husband," NIV).

- Developing admiration. You have a one-of-a-kind man, so discover who your husband is and communicate the discovery. Find his good qualities. Do not try to discover the qualities of other women's husbands.
- Develop mutual interests. Minimize your personal interests and maximize your mutual interests.

Illustration: Shared Interests

A couple divorced. He said his first wife had no interest in the things he liked. His second wife did things he liked.

In the case of another couple, he loved sports. She knew nothing about sports, so she watched sports with him and learned to do needlework while watching sports on television with him.

- Have a good listening ear. Be vitally interested in what he shares with you.
- Do you treat him as the most special and prized person in the world?
- Look for his good character traits to admire.
- Do not interrupt his stories and tell them better than he does, even if you can.
- Learn to accept his feelings, his tastes, his attitudes, and his differences.
- Forget the past. Forgive his wrongs, his errors, his failures, and his sins.
- Respect his decisions, his methods, and his opinions. See his motives behind these. (Many problems with which couples struggle are based on a "You do it one way" and "I do it another way" mentality. Instead, think, "What value is it in eternity?")
- Notice his actions, his physique, and his appearance.
- Avoid being quarrelsome toward your husband.
  o Proverbs 21:9 – "Better to live on a corner of the roof than share a house with a quarrelsome wife" (NIV).
  o Proverbs 19:13 – "A foolish child is a father's ruin, and a quarrelsome wife is like the constant dripping of a leaky roof" (NIV).

The Wife's Needs

Consider these statements:

1. In a marriage, men and women are equal; however, in a marriage, men and women have distinct and separate functions.

2. The wife is to submit to her husband.
    *   A submissive wife can win her husband over without words.
        *   1 Peter 3:1 – "Wives, in the same way submit yourselves to your own husbands so that, if any of them do not believe the word, they may be won over without words by the behavior of their wives" (NIV).
    *   A wife should submit to her husband as her husband submits to God.
        *   1 Corinthians 11:3 – "But I want you to realize that the head of every man is Christ, and the head of the woman is man, and the head of Christ is God" (NIV).
    *   It is not a comparison nor a compromise, but a submission.
    *   They are joined together as one, a union.

- o Genesis 2:24 – "That is why a man leaves his father and mother and is united to his wife, and they become one flesh" (NIV).
- They are joined physically, emotionally, spiritually, and mentally.
- They are to love each other, live with each other, support each other, and talk to each other.
- She is a helper suitable for him. She is comparable to him. The wife is a helper; she should not compete with her husband. She is his "Ebenezer" (see 1 Samuel 7:12). She should not try to be the voice of the Holy Spirit but be her husband's helper.
  - o Genesis 2:18b – The Lord God said, "… I will make a helper suitable for him" (NIV).
- God said, "It is good… It is very good," in His creation; however, when He created man, He said, "It is not good for the man to be alone" (Genesis 2:18a, NIV). A husband or a wife may not want sex because they do not feel connected. Men connect more emotionally with sex, whereas women connect more emotionally with foreplay and intimacy. Husbands and wives must find creative ways to connect with each other emotionally.
3. All women need the following:

- To be accepted (as they are) and to be known individually
- To be understood
- To have other female relationships (sisterhood)
- To express deep emotions at times

Answer the following questions.

1. Do I know my husband's needs? Do I know my wife's needs? Make a list of the needs of your spouse, discuss your lists, and discover how you can help each other if possible. Some needs are in God's hands.
2. Make a commitment to meet the needs of your mate as much as you can.

Illustration: *A Divorced Couple*

A couple got a divorce. Her reason for the divorce: "We never go anywhere together!" His reason: "I work long hours. When do we have time to go?"

Proper Drainage: Devaluing Your Mate Causes Injuries

In building a house, it is important to install the proper drainage system so water will flow freely through the pipes. In a marriage, communication flows when husbands and wives value their mates instead of allowing devaluing habits to develop. Valuing each other will bring joy in the journey of day-to-day living.

When the Husband Devalues His Wife

Devaluing a wife occurs when a husband fails to notice his wife, her house décor, her organization and cleaning, and other things she oversees. When he fails to appreciate what she does, or he fails to appreciate and value what she says, he devalues her. He underestimates small things, but they are big things to her. She hears and feels words that hurt.

- Psalm 141:3 – "Set a guard over my mouth, Lord; keep watch over the door of my lips" (NIV).

He devalues her by speaking to her in harsh tones or with a loud volume, or he talks down to her, treating her like a child.

He devalues her by correcting her (in rude tones) while she is talking or interrupting her with his own plans or ideas as if hers are not important to him. He should listen to her. He devalues her when he corrects her in the presence of others. Most husbands know when their wives are smarter than they are. He devalues her when he cuts her out of the discussion or conversation, even when she does not understand.

The husband devalues his wife when he acts suspicious (sometimes protecting her), such as hiding information from her, protecting his calendar or schedule, and hiding or putting a hidden code on his cell phone. When he knows something hurts her and will not tell her, she might suspect something.

A husband devalues his wife when he admires another woman over her. A glance becomes a stare when he does it all the time. It is okay to notice an attractive woman, but to keep his focus on her is not complimentary to his wife. Plus, the woman he is staring at notices it and knows of his visual disloyalty. A husband should pray for God to guard his eyes.

- Psalm 141:8-9 – "But my eyes are fixed on you, Sovereign Lord; in you I take refuge—do not give me over to death. Keep me safe from the traps set by evildoers, from the snares they have laid for me" (NIV).

When the wife sees the husband looking at other women, she is easily bruised by the man she loves. Women are very discerning and sensitive.

Illustration: *Eyes Forward*

A woman hit her husband over the head with a skillet. He asked her why she did it, and she said she found a woman's name in his pocket. He said, "Oh, that, it is a racehorse's name." The next day, she hit him with a larger skillet, and again, he asked why. She said, "Your horse just called on the phone and asked for you."

When a husband devalues his wife, it may be due to self-centeredness.

Devaluation comes when a husband ignores his wife's conversation by not listening.

Illustration: *Are You Listening?*

When the wife thought her husband was not listening, she changed the subject and began a new conversation about an unrelated topic: "When the monkey in our backyard was climbing a tree ..." It usually made the husband realize he was not listening.

Devaluation comes when we are not thankful. Find things to be thankful for in your journey. Sometimes bad manners and an ungrateful and unthankful heart can lead to divorce. There is power in a grateful heart.

- Psalm 34:1-3 – "I will extol the Lord at all times; his praise will always be on my lips. I will glory in the Lord; let the afflicted hear and rejoice. Glorify the Lord with me; let us exalt his name together" (NIV).

When the Wife Devalues Her Husband

A wife devalues her husband when she puts him down in front of others or makes fun of his weaknesses.

She devalues him when she does things behind his back (like when she fixes what he has already done). The man is a "fixer," so she should just show appreciation and let the imperfectly fixed things go.

The wife devalues her husband when she constantly badgers or nags him for not doing what she wants. An alternative is to make a Honey Do list and post it (make it a beautiful piece of artwork). Then, brag on him and compliment him when something is completed on the Honey Do list.

She devalues him when she uses the phrases "You *always* do …" or "You *never* do …" about things when she is not pleased.

Illustration: *No Nagging!*

If the husband says he will fix it, he will fix it! The wife does not have to remind him six months later.

She devalues her husband when she holds him responsible for her emotional bad moods. Also, she devalues him when she does not tell him why she is in a bad mood, but makes him think it is his fault. She can also hold him responsible for her emotional strength.

When the wife complains about what they do not have or what they cannot get regarding material things, she devalues her husband. The husband is a provider, so he will try to get what she wants, whether they need it or not or can afford it or not. She should be content.

Illustration: *The Washing Machine*
The husband is fixing the washing machine. He has been in the garage for a long time. The wife looks in, and he is on the floor with parts all around him. They decided to save and buy a new washing machine.

Illustration: *The Necklaces*

The wife admires two necklaces at a craft show. She cannot decide which one to buy. She laid aside both necklaces because they could not afford either of them. When she got home, her husband gave her the gift of both necklaces—a love gift to say, "I love you."

She devalues him when she does not appreciate his efforts and does not value what he does. A man's ego is tied to his wife. The wife can easily hurt him by not valuing his efforts, his opinions, or his gifts. All injuries hurt when a person is self-centered.

A wife does not have to change her husband's mind even if she does not agree with him. She can just say, "I may be wrong, but I think I am right." When a wife disagrees and there is no way out, just be quiet and let the husband be right.

- James 3:16 – "For where you have envy and selfish ambition, there you find disorder and every evil practice" (NIV).

A wife and a husband can waste their time, or they can invest in their life and improve them. What are you investing in, and who are you investing in? A person knows he or she has forgiven someone if he or she has a chance to retaliate in words or deeds but chooses not to react in this way.

A wife devalues her husband when she criticizes, belittles, or puts him down. Praise your husband. Praise him especially in front of others. Never talk about your intimate life to others. Never say anything questionable or bad about him to others. This is loyalty and respect.

A wife devalues her husband when she does not commit to his needs. Accept his sexual needs and let him know you accept his needs. Be more sexual than you feel. Men are more visually oriented.

A wife devalues her husband when she does not treat him as her friend. Be his buddy. When you are your husband's friend, you should participate with him and do things he enjoys.

- Learn to love what he loves.
- Learn how to share his world.

Illustration: *Learning to Crochet*

When my husband and I married, I had no idea that he was into watching sports so strongly. I was not athletically inclined; however, he had been a star football player in both high school and college. He had received football scholarships, which paid for his entire college education. So, when I discovered that he wanted to watch a lot of sports, I realized I needed to support his interests; therefore, I learned to watch the games with him and go to football games and ask him questions about the plays. One time a player threw a football almost the total length of the field for a touchdown.... It was such an incredible play that I jumped up and started cheering his super wonderful play. My sweet husband pulled my arm and told me to sit down as I was cheering for the wrong team!

Answer the following questions.

1. List ways that you may be devaluing your spouse. List ways your spouse may be devaluing you. Exchange lists and, with humility, discuss these lists in peace. Discuss how you can affirm each other more in the future and list the actions you need to take.

2. Use the strengths list and find your own strengths and weaknesses. Use your strengths to enhance your marriage. Help each other in the areas of weakness. Remember, God usually puts opposites together.

Interior Decorations for the Home: Positive Affirmation

Just as a designer selects the best decorations for a home, so too a couple should commit to building up and affirming the beautiful qualities in each other and to enjoy the adornments of agape love.

Consider the following list of ways to affirm your spouse:

1. Affirm your spouse's identity.
2. Affirm your spouse's intelligence. Be careful about your influence and what you say so that you are not putting down your spouse.
3. Affirm your spouse's individuality. Be your mate's cheerleader and champion. Compliment your spouse's hair, hands, eyes, and tell your spouse he or she is "altogether lovely."
4. Be a complimentary person.
5. Be a friend and learn how to relax with your spouse. What is your spouse's love language (Chapman, 2015)?

6. Affirm your spouse's character. Use affirming words; note his or her strengths; and love, comfort, and respect your spouse.

7. Be friends. Affirm your friendship with your spouse. Song of Solomon 2:16a: "My beloved is mine and I am my beloved's" (NIV). Resource: *Staying In Love for a Lifetime* (2001) by Ed Wheat and Gloria Okes Perkins.

8. Honor your spouse. You are either honoring or dishonoring each other.

9. Honor and respect will build a strong foundation. Pray this: "God help me to honor my true love." The wife should honor and reverence her husband as the leader of the family. She should treat him like a king, no matter how he acts. And the husband should love his wife as Christ loved the Church.

   - Other words for *reverence*: admire, adore, appreciate, cherish, defer, esteem, honor, notice, prize, regard, respect, treasure, value. Ephesians 5:33 – "However, each one of you must love his wife as he loves himself, and the wife must respect (reverence) her husband" (NIV).

10. The husband has the responsibility to work and provide the finances for the family, the responsibility of leadership, and the responsibility for the care and protection of each

family member. The wife should submit to her husband's leadership with love.

11. The wife is responsible as the homemaker to take care of the children; to keep up the house; to do the cooking, cleaning, washing clothes, and other household chores; and to be her husband's helpmate.

- Genesis 2:18, 20b-24 – The Lord God said, "It is not good for the man to be alone. I will make a helper suitable for him." … So the Lord God caused the man to fall into a deep sleep; and … he took one of the man's ribs and … made a woman from the rib … and he brought her to the man. The man said, "This is now bone of my bones and flesh of my flesh; she shall be called 'woman,' for she was taken out of man." That is why a man leaves his father and mother and is united to his wife, and they become one flesh" (NIV).

If she works outside the home, a plan should be in place to help her with her household responsibilities.

1. The wife is her husband's helper, and the two shall become one.

- John 17:20-21 – "My prayer is not for them alone. I pray also for those who will believe in me through their message, that all of them may be one, Father, just as you are in me and I am in you. May they also be in us so that the world may believe that you have sent me" (NIV).

What do couples do when they both need to work outside the home for finances? Consider ways you can support each other in this circumstance.

2. Love is security and strength. Strength and stubbornness, or strength and stability. True love never lets go of the loved one. (See 1 Corinthians 13.)
3. The sacrifice of love is self-control and selflessness.
4. Do not eclipse the marital relationship. Let the husband and the wife discover each other. Resource: How to Save Your Marriage Alone (1983) by Ed Wheat.
5. The wife should make the husband feel like a man by being 100% a woman. Likewise, the husband should make the wife feel like a woman by being 100% a man.

Illustration: *Letting Yourself "Go to Pot"*

In some marriages, husbands may neglect to express their love to their wives, or wives may fail to express their reverence and respect for their husbands. When this happens, spouses may stop caring about their bodies and let themselves "go to pot." They may gain weight because they have lost the desire to work on their marriages.

Love is not just an emotion; love is an agape commitment.

If the grass looks greener on the other side … you may need to water and fertilize your side. If the grass looks greener on the other side … perhaps you cannot see the trash and debris on the other side.

Emotions come and go. Men tend to feel like emotions accumulate and work on a point system. For example, they may think they earn points for bringing their wives flowers, a box of candy, or jewelry; by taking their wives on trips or out to dinner; or by doing house cleaning, yardwork, or shopping. Men feel these points add up, but women go day by day, and every day is a new day. For women, past points do not accumulate, nor do they carry over.

Answer the following questions.

1. How can I affirm my mate more? List ways you can show more positive affirmation, and determine the best ways to put this affirmation into action.

2. Work on affirmation of your spouse's identity, intelligence, individuality, character, words, and emotional personality.

3. Define agape love and commitment. Do we have an agape commitment in our marriage?

4. What is my spouse's love language?

5. Which describes our marriage: (1) Strength and stubbornness, or (2) Strength and stability. Discuss.

Paint the Interior to Suit the Homeowner: Submission

The builder should seek to understand the owner's preferences. A husband and a wife should seek to understand one another: "However, each one of you also must love his wife as he loves himself, and the wife must respect her husband" **(Ephesians 5:33, NIV).**

Be subject or submit to one another. The world is filled with rebellion. Watchman Nee states, "Now we see the spirit of the Antichrist working everywhere. The most prominent feature of Antichrist is lawlessness (i.e., rebellion)" (The Bible – Recovery Version, n.d., ch. 9, "The seventy weeks in Daniel," para. 8).

A wife should be submissive to her husband as unto the Lord. Submission is a service to God. A woman should not see submission to her husband as a negative factor; she should see it as an opportunity to show her love to the Lord and see it as submission to God. Agape love is godly love, not emotional love. Agape love is a deep, God-honoring commitment of the will. The husband should display mutual submission to his wife.

Illustration: *Finances*

After several years of marriage, my husband and I were getting deeper and deeper into debt. Finally, our finances were a mess. We knew a man trained in the Larry Burkett financial management plans, and we invited him to train us. After watching a video on applying biblical financial principles, the counselor began to reveal how to get our finances back in good condition. Since my husband was a spender and I was a saver, I thought the man would address my husband on how we needed to save. He began to read John 17, Jesus' prayer. I thought, as he began reading the passage, "Oh, boy, now he is going to let my husband have it! Wow, this is great! He will tell my husband how wrong he is and how right I am in my 'saving attitude.'"

To my surprise, instead, he brought out how Jesus was ONE with the Father, and so we needed to be one in our finances. With that statement, I was immediately under conviction that I needed to be one with my husband. In saving money, I needed to be more flexible, and my husband needed to be more intentional, so we could be one in our marriage. We submitted to one another and became one in our finances!

- Ephesians 5:21 – "Submit to one another out of reverence for Christ" (NIV).

Life is doing what God says and not what you want to do. If you want answers to prayers, your first responsibility is to submit to God as your authority and have a goal of unity and a closer walk with the Lord in your individual life.

- Colossians 3:23-24 – "Whatever you do, work at it with all your heart, as working for the Lord, not for human masters It is the Lord Christ you are serving" (NIV).
- Be sensitive to the Holy Spirit.
- Seek to please and edify the Lord and your spouse.
- Choose to work together in spite of your differences.

Marriage is an everyday event, and so we need to work on our marriage every day. Two options: (1) You can be stressed out until you fall apart; or (2) You can be stressed out and accept peace and have a quiet heart that casts out cares but not responsibilities.

- 1 Peter 5:7 – "Cast all your anxiety on him because he cares for you" (NIV).

Marriage is a picture of Christ and the Church. How does this relationship picture Christ and the Church? Why is Christ the groom of the Church and the Church the Bride of Christ?

Submission is an attitude of the heart. True submission to God leads to much less harassment from Satan. Trust the Holy Spirit to be your Guide.

- 1 Peter 3:1-2 – "Wives, in the same way submit yourselves to your own husbands so that, if any of them do not believe the word, they may be won over without words by the behavior of their wives, when they see the purity and reverence of your lives" (NIV).

A couple begins a project together. He decides to do things his way, but she has a better plan to do the same job. They argue … have a big disagreement … and the only way out is for one to yield! The question is, which way is the right way? Most of the time, God does not mind which way you choose.

Illustration: *The Porch and the Garden Design*

A couple was sitting on their porch, and the gardener was working in the flower bed. The gardener asked them to choose one of two designs. The husband wanted the flower bed planted symmetrically, and the wife wanted an asymmetrical design. When no decision was made and the disagreement was mounting, the gardener asked, "Who spends more time on the porch looking at the plants?" The wife won because she sat on the porch every day, and her husband seldom sat on the porch.

How do you get to the place where submission is easy? Joyce Meyer states, "Stop the flesh and increase the spirit little by little" (Soldier of God – Meyer, 2022).

The highest form of worship is total submission. The submission of a wife is essential because God has chosen the husband to be the leader in a marriage. Both should submit to one another on issues, but the order of authority places God first, with the husband directly responsible to God.

- Ephesians 5:25-27 – "Husbands, love your wives, just as Christ loved the church and gave himself up for her to make her holy, cleansing her by the washing with water through the word, and to present her to himself as a radiant church, without stain or wrinkle or any other blemish, but holy and blameless" (NIV).
- Submission helps your husband change.
- Submission affirms and edifies your husband.
- Submission allows God to use your obedience to settle controversial issues.

Honor your husband in his potential (even if he has not yet reached or has only partially reached his potential). Constantly think about the best quality in your husband and praise him for that character trait and his application of it. To your husband, speak his positive, potential destiny.

Husbands want their wives to be their friends, and they want them to be fun.

- Come out of your world and into his world. Open your heart to him.
- Husbands need their wives to tell them how they feel. Do not expect your husband to read your thoughts.
- Meet the needs of your spouse's sexual life. Men need sexual touching, and they are visual. Operative sexual intimacy and betterment take time. Communication for intimacy is 7% words, 55% body expression, and 38% voice tone (Luna, 2020, para. 3).
- Practice domestic support at home; pick up after yourself.
- Women practice "nesting."
- Everyone should do their part.
- Wives can honor their husbands with simple things: nourish them, care for them, and comfort them.

Equality in marriage. Everything a husband and wife do, they do together. Do not isolate from one another. Do not forsake and abandon your spouse. Almost all adultery is emotional abandonment.

- Hebrews 13:5b – "Never will I leave you; never will I forsake you" (NIV).

Praise and compliment your husband. Forget his faults by complimenting his good points. Encourage him to do right instead of fussing, nagging, and complaining about his faults. As the saying goes, "Anything you can feed, you can train."

- Proverbs 31:10 – "A wife of noble character who can find? She is worth far more than rubies" (NIV).
- Philippians 2:13 – "… it is God who works in you to will and to act in order to fulfill his good purpose" (NIV).

Answer the following questions.

1. What is our definition of submission?
2. In what ways or areas do I need to improve my total submission to both God and to my spouse?
3. Is our marriage a picture of Christ and the Church?
4. For what and how can I praise my spouse?
5. Is there a difference between "honor" and "submission"?
6. If we find two ways to do a project, which one of us needs to submit? Why?
7. What ways can we discern how to do more *fun* activities together?
8. Am I a *complainer* or am I a *praiser* to my spouse?

Homeowner Preferences: Priorities in a Marriage

Homeowners choose design elements and paint selections to enhance the beauty and attraction of the home. More importantly, though, the true environment of the home stems from couples setting priorities in their day-to-day schedules, giving attention to time and family needs.

Consider the following list:

1. Work on your marriage.
   - Date every week. Make this once-a-week special time a top priority. You do not have to spend much money. You can picnic, drive through a scenic area, or go fishing.

Illustration: *Make a List*

After our first date, my future husband asked where we should go on our second date. I said, "I don't know. I can think of lots of places for us to go." Since he was in school and working part time and I just barely knew him, I was not sure how much he could spend on a date. He responded jokingly, "Make a list, and I will call you." Because I was interested in dating him, I made a list of 100 non-costly things to do. When he called me, I was ready with my list.

- Every four to six weeks, spend some extended time alone with each other and talk about goals, ambitions, desires, needs, problems, and other things. Spend time without distractions.
  - o 1 Corinthians 7:35 – "I am saying this for your own good, not to restrict you, but that you may live in a right way in undivided devotion to the Lord" (NIV).
  - o For that time alone, talk to each other for an agreed-upon amount of uninterrupted time.
- We all have the same amount of time. We either invest our time or we waste our time.
  - o Psalm 90:10-12 – "Our days may come to seventy years, or eighty, if our strength endures; yet the best of them are but trouble and sorrow, for they quickly pass, and we fly away. If only we knew the power of your anger! Your wrath is as great as the fear that is your due. Teach us to number our days, that we may gain a heart of wisdom" (NIV).

Illustration: *Mary and Martha*

Mary sat at the feet of Jesus and just listened to Him, whereas Martha was busy doing the necessary household food preparations. What Jesus was saying is, "We do need to do necessary chores, but also, we need to sit at the feet of Jesus and gain our spiritual strength, too." (See Luke 10:38-42.)

- Philippians 2:14 – "Do everything without grumbling or arguing" (NIV).

Women set the attitude, atmosphere, and mood of their home.

- Do some activity together.
- Do some type of physical touch in the morning and in the evening.
- Do something unexpected.
- When huge problems come, spend seven days working on solving the problem together.
- Seek wisdom and counsel when needed. The shortest distance between two points is a straight line.
  - Proverbs 11:14 – "For lack of guidance a nation falls, but victory is won through many advisers" (NIV).

2. Share everything.
   - Each spouse's parents are important, and children are important and should be considered, but mate time is a top priority.

Illustration: *Mate Time*

Cleave and leave. Some spouses put their <u>parents</u> as their top priority over their mates and spend too much time pleasing their parents. Some spouses put their <u>children</u> as their top priority over their mates and spend too much time pleasing their children. Remember, after your relationship with the Lord, your spouse is your top priority.

- All decisions should be made as a family, together and united. All are one.

- When the children are grown and married, the spouses that have put each other as top priority over the years, usually have a more lasting oneness in their marriage.

3. Family needs.
   - Devotionals

   - Work

   - Entertainment

   - Play

   - Rest

4. Things that steal family time:
   - Excess work. Being a workaholic can negatively impact family time.

   - People pleasers. Prune off some of the demands of others when these impinge upon family time.

- Hindrances. Locate any hindrances and prioritize family time.

Answer the following questions.

1. What are some ways we can improve our marriage? What are our priorities in our marriage upon which we can agree? Do we have a special date and time set aside on a regular basis?

2. What are some of our together time goals? (For example, a couple has extremely stressful jobs; they made a covenant not to bring work problems home.) After your relationship with the Lord, make your spousal relationship your top priority.

3. Is our schedule allowing us to meet our marriage needs as well as our family time needs? Where can we improve our priorities?

4. Make a list of low-cost or no-cost things we can do together as a couple.

5. Have we set aside time to evaluate our directions in life?

Final Plans: Problems in a Marriage

Final ideas are executed in building the home, such as making choices regarding furniture, kitchen appliances, and other things; and the homeowners should be in agreement so as not to cause problems. When couples work together in unity, many problems can be solved.

Some things can cause stress in a marriage. Spouses need validation when things are tough. Stress factors can include the following:

- Rules, rewards, punishments, and responsibilities for children
- Money, what to buy, when to buy, how much to spend, and differences in how both spouses were raised regarding money values
- Sex problems
- Workplace, how much to discuss at home, how much to leave at work

- House and yard, who is responsible for what and when and to what degree of organization

Illustration: *Responsibilities of Mates*

Early in our marriages, couples should decide who is responsible for the household, yard, car, and other areas so they can each be responsible for chores and duties around the house. This helps couples not to blame each other when a job needs to be done.

Healthy families do not deny their problems by "sweeping them under the rug."

A couple needs to have a clear understanding of what the problem or problems are.

- James 1:22-25 – "Do not merely listen to the word, and so deceive yourselves. Do what it says. Anyone who listens to the word but does not do what it says is like someone who looks at his face in a mirror and, after looking at himself, goes away and immediately forgets what he looks like. But whoever looks intently into the perfect law that gives freedom, and continues in it—not forgetting what they have heard, but doing it—they will be blessed in what they do" (NIV).

A couple should recognize the problem or problems and identify the need for improvement and try to solve them. Desire for change comes from inner motivation, and then comes a commitment to change. Each person must submit, yield, and adapt with a learner's heart. Then comes obedience, a plan of action, and completing the project of solving the situation.

Illustration: *Areas of Improvement*

As mentioned earlier, in our marriage, my husband and I discovered we had five problem areas. Instead of solving them, we just swept them under the rug. Then, our rug became so bumpy that we could not walk on it. We had to learn how to deal with each problem and, instead of just passing over it, find a solution that was agreeable to both of us.

Unresolved problems of a couple can be internalized by a child. These problems may come out years later as anger, bitterness, or rebellion.

Denial does not eliminate the pain.

- Ephesians 4:24 – "… put on the new self, created to be like God in true righteousness and holiness" (NIV).

A person in denial does not admit that there is a problem. A person in denial makes excuses. (Example: Adam and Eve, Genesis 3.)

Be open, honest, and confront denial.

- Openness requires love.
- Create safety zones or limits to sharing. People need to share what is hurting.
- Develop a prayer partnership.

Illustration: *Martin and Mary*

When a couple married after their first spouses had died, they wanted to keep an open and honest relationship, so they set up a daily habit of reading some Scripture, discussing the passage, and then praying together. This really helped them to develop a close-knit marriage.

- Construct a place of protection for prayer.
- Find a new freedom and put off fears.

Mate validation. "My emotions are real; they may not be right, but they are still real to me."

Illustration: *Newly Married*

A couple was newly married and the husband, formerly a widower, had left everything from his former marriage in the house. It was not a style of furniture that the new wife liked, and so she proceeded to sell everything, including the antique furniture, without his permission. He did not want it changed! They divorced because he was still emotionally attached to his first wife and her tastes.

- A husband or wife validates his or her spouse by saying, "Are you okay?"
- Sit down and say:
  - "Am I doing alright?"
  - "How can I improve?"
  - "What do I need to do to improve?"
  - "I care about your emotions. Right or wrong, they are real."

One by one, every problem has a solution with God's help. "A cord of three strands is not quickly broken" (Ecclesiastes 4:12, NIV).

Do these things to support good problem-solving in a marriage:

1. Tell the *truth* in love (Ephesians 4:15).
2. *Listen*: The first duty of love is to listen.
3. Plan a good time for *communication.* If one person is an early riser and the other needs coffee before waking up, plan a time that will work for both.
4. *Kindness*: Do not raise your voice. Express yourself lovingly.

5. Allow for *thinking time*: You have shared; let your mate have time to think it through. You may let the person start all over. Some people are "thinkers" and need time to process the problem and to process solutions, too.

6. *Pray* together and pray for each other. It is hard to pray for someone and stay mad at them.

7. *Pursue* the *important* and *urgent* issues in marriage:

    • What is urgent should not supersede what is important. In most cases, a spouse tends to focus on the urgent to the neglect of the important.

    • Finances are important. Consider these four possibilities:
        o Important and Urgent
        o Important and Not Urgent
        o Urgent but Not Important
        o Not Important and Not Urgent

    • Health is important. Emergencies in health issues are both urgent and important.

    • Our walk with God is important.

Answer the following questions.

1. Do we have a clear plan as to who is responsible for what in our home (garage, car, appliances, income taxes, checkbook, fixing things)?

2. Do we have a transparent relationship in which we can discuss our feelings, emotions, and fears and still be friends? Are we close enough that we can be honest in communicating?

3. Do we have a clear understanding of the differences between important issues and urgent issues?

4. Do we work at creating solutions to our problems? Do we let them go or sweep them under the rug?

5. Am I in denial that we have some problems? Am I willing to admit my denial and work with my spouse to find solutions?

Repair Problems: Guard Against Destructive Factors

After a home is built, eventually repairs will be needed. In a marriage, allowing strife, lack of self-control, and other factors can be destructive. Guard your marriage.

Strife in the home equals rebellion in the children. Be redemptive. Pursue marriage above the church; pursue marriage above your children; and pursue marriage above your job.

God has given each of us the same amount of grace. We are given grace for what we need to do.

- Ephesians 4:7 – "But to each one of us grace has been given as Christ apportioned it" (NIV).

We are given unity even with all of the family diversity.

The fruit of self-control. When you are angry or mad, you do not have the privilege of responding to the way you feel if you want to be sold out to God. Try to think before you respond, and let your response be a reply that has a sweet tone and a ton of love.

Keep strife out of your life. Keep strife out of your ministry. Keep strife out of your home. According to Steven Furtick, "'Offense' is an event, but 'offended' is a decision" (2016, Elevation Church, 43:08). Sometimes strife comes from others who are immature or sensitive. If that happens, you may have to do some quick thinking, praying, and listening to the Lord before you respond. During an argument, do not respond to anger with anger.

Illustration: *Golf Course*

My husband and I, at one point in our marriage, had an area of a battlefield. I did not understand his anger over the problem, so I responded with returned anger. This problem area lasted for a long time, and there seemed to be no answer. It was a hurtful situation, so one day, I walked across a golf course near our house late in the evening when there were no golfers. I cried and talked to the Lord and asked Him to help us solve this problem. God showed me that I was responding in anger to his anger. I asked God to help me. So later, when we got into that same argumentative stage of this problem again, I responded in anger to his anger. Then, I remembered, I was not supposed to respond in anger. I prayed and asked God to help me be more aware of my responses. The next time we hit that topic, and he was angry, I stopped in the middle of my angered response and shut my mouth. I prayed again for victory, and then, the next time, I did not respond in anger. My husband noticed my change in attitude, that I did not respond in anger, so he talked to a friend about his feelings related to the problem. We, finally, were able to solve the problem and eliminate our angered responses.

Five things that can destroy a marriage:

1. *Defensiveness.* Talk over the problems. Validate what your spouse says. Listen and seek to understand your spouse's viewpoint. It may take lots of questions and listening for you to understand, but it will be worth the effort. It is okay to explain your actions when you are defending a misunderstanding.

2. *Criticism.* If you accidentally say one bad thing, turn things around and say ten good things. Try to see what your mate is saying by responding, "When you said that, this is the way I heard it, or this is the way I feel."

3. *Controlling or domineering attitude.* No one controls anything in a marriage. We are equal in a marriage. Everything we do, we do together as one half of a whole apple.

4. *Isolation.* Do not forsake and abandon your spouse. Emotional abandonment feels like adultery.

5. Hebrews 13:5b – "Never will I leave you; never will I forsake you" (NIV).

6. *Not communicating the truth.* We need to always communicate the truth (not untruths or half-truths).

Answer the following questions.

1. Are we exhibiting any of the five factors that can destroy a marriage?

   - Defensiveness
   - Criticism
   - Controlling or domineering attitude
   - Isolation
   - Lack of communicating the truth

2. In which of these areas do we need to find immediate solutions?

Fix the Leaky Roof: Solving Problems

Many times, a house with small repair needs, such as fixing a leaky roof or putting screws into a latch on the screen door, is neglected for some time and can create further problems. In the same way, couples can help alleviate annoying habits, quarrels, or poor attitudes before they become enormous irritants by solving small problems in a marriage quickly.

(This section contains ideas from previously covered material. Small problems need repeated work.)

The wife needs to stay on one topic when discussing family needs and problems and not try to discuss 30 different topics. The husband is more single-minded and focused than his wife. He stays on one topic and deals with that issue until it is settled. Spare the details; men do not like the details. Women speak 25,000 words per day; men speak 10,000. The wife does not use her words during the day at home. The husband may have used his 10,000 at work.

Stop giving your husband advice and stop giving him driving instructions.

- Matthew 5:9 – "Blessed are the peacemakers, for they will be called children of God" (NIV).

You do not have to have the last word. You are not your spouse's teacher, nor the Holy Spirit's voice, nor the Holy Spirit's interpreter.

Be teachable and willing to say, "I might be wrong," even when you know you are right, or be willing to apologize. "I might be wrong" is a stress reliever.

Wives, trust in God and submit to your husbands. The wife's failure is the husband's failure. (See Proverbs 31.) The wife wants to be led by the husband through his leadership, and she wants him to pursue her. She does not want to be bullied by dominance. A husband does not need to demand and dominate just because he is the leader.

Concentrate on being the right mate rather than trying to change your spouse. Instead, change yourself. Resource: *Lord, Change Me* (2008) by Evelyn Christenson.

We want something, but we do not want to do what we should do to get what we desire. "I know myself and my worldview, but I do not see yours." You cannot erase what you have said, but you can replace what you see in others' views.

Is my spouse more beautiful because of me, or am I destroying him/her?

- Proverbs 14:1 – "The wise woman builds her house, but the foolish tears it down with her own hands" (NASB). Or vice versa.
- 1 Peter 3:4 – "Rather, it should be that of your inner self, the unfading beauty of a gentle and quiet spirit, which is of great worth in God's sight" (NIV).

God created us for marriage. We must take responsibility.

- Proverbs 16:9 – "In their hearts humans plan their course, but the Lord establishes their steps" (NIV).
- Spouses must have redemptive love for each other. Because of differences in couples' ways and personalities, we should respond in love to problems and have patience in solving them.

Mates should be consistent and real. Compliment before you criticize. Notice actions, physique, and appearance. Give your spouse a pep rally, if needed. Compliment and appreciate your spouse instead of comparing him or her to another person. Love even when your spouse is wrong!

- Proverbs 19:13b – "A quarrelsome wife is like the constant dripping of a leaky roof" (NIV).
- Proverbs 21:9 – "Better to live on a corner of the roof than share a house with a quarrelsome wife" (NIV).

God puts no limit on what a woman can do. Love is doing or saying, or being something to show your admiration and respect. Love is action.

- Proverbs 31:10 – "A wife of noble character who can find? She is worth far more than rubies" (NIV).

You may make suggestions. This does not mean advising, conniving, and deceiving by playing on your spouse's emotions; nor does it mean griping, murmuring, grumbling, disputing, maneuvering, or arguing. Sometimes the motivation for change can be one of these:

- Habits are irritating.
- Self-righteous attitudes are hard to deal with.
- For his or her benefit, improve in some area.

Check your motivations and allow God to change your spouse.

Illustration: *Four-Paned Window*

Using the visual of a window with four panes, we can discuss visual perception and intellectual perception:

Answer the following questions.

1. If we discover one or some of these destroyers in our lives, are we willing to receive God's help in overcoming them?

2. Sometimes we need an emotional perception of the other person's feelings or point of view. We may need an intellectual perception of each other's desires, direction, or goals. "Am I willing to ask?

   - "I might be wrong. Have I misunderstood the problem?"

   - "Forgive me for … Is this what you are trying to say to me? Let me hear what you are trying to say."

   - Am I willing to let go and allow my spouse to have the last word?

3. Am I consistently admiring, showing respect for, and noticing my spouse, and do I complement my spouse in some way?

4. Do I have irritating habits I can change?

5. Am I a negative person in any of these areas?

   - Deceiving or lying

   - Disputing or murmuring

   - Arguing or being irritating

- Grumbling or griping
- Self-righteousness, pride, or arrogance
- Conniving or maneuvering
- Other

Making Changes: Both the Husband and the Wife

[This section is adapted from a sermon by John Hagee and Matt Hagee.]

Just like a building needs changes from time to time, a marriage can benefit from making changes.

Things men need to know:

Men need to have confidence in knowing God, placing their faith in God, and being faithful to their commitment to God.

- Men must have confidence before commitment. Hold on until the end. Real men do not quit.
  - Hebrews 3:14 – "We have come to share in Christ, if indeed we hold our original conviction firmly to the very end" (NIV).
  - A real man has a godly source of counsel. Be a good counselor, but have a good source of counsel.
  - Proverbs 11:14 – "For lack of guidance a nation falls, but victory is won through many advisers" (NIV).

- Be concerned and express feelings. Real men have feelings, a heart filled with love; be willing to express your feelings.
- A husband must love his wife with understanding.
- Communication. Do not be afraid to tell others how you feel, and be sure to tell your family how you feel. Communicate, not dictate.
- Courage. Have a willingness to face your fears. Look at fears and see them. Turn to the Lord with your fears and do not live with fear and hurt in your heart.
  - Psalm 34:4 – "I sought the Lord, and he answered me; he delivered me from all my fears" (NIV).

Things women need to know:

Women need to face their fears, too. Women need to be consistent.

- Give up the unreal expectations of both yourself and your spouse. Giving up your expectations is yielding or submitting to the Holy Spirit.
- Esteem each other as higher than yourselves.

Things couples need to know:

You cannot *control* people. You cannot *change* people. You should not judge people. Sometimes you make assumptions about another person's motives for doing something. Many problems are related to one person assuming his or her mate's motive for some action. Then, the first person, with a wrong assumption about the motive, gets angry, upset, or irritated and explodes, or may accuse his or her mate without knowing the facts or motive. You cannot know your spouse's motive unless you ask. Then, you need to believe what your spouse said was his or her motive is really the truth. Right or wrong, a motive must be respected even when it hurts. Talking over motives can save a lot of friction and problems. So what do you do? Billy Graham says, "From our hearts come our motives, our desires, our goals, our emotions. If the heart is right, then the actions will be right" (2006, p. 253).

Yield control and surrender your will. Let it go, and let God do the changing.

Love rather than trying to control, change, or judge the person.

- Pray for and declare divine intervention.
- Do not fear; God is with you.
    - o 2 Timothy 1:7 – "For God has not given us a spirit of fear, but of power and of love and of a sound mind" (NKJV).
    - o Make preparations for the future on a positive note.
    - o Work on core values.

Answer the following questions.

1. Am I willing to accept my mate unconditionally? Am I willing to surrender and yield control of my will to God, seeking divine intervention and listening to what the Holy Spirit says?

2. Do I have unreal expectations? Am I willing to yield these expectations to God?

3. In what ways am I esteeming my spouse?

4. Do I have any problems with trying to control things? Am I willing to let it go?

5. Do I make assumptions about my spouse's motives for doing things or saying things, possibly based on my need to control or change my spouse? Am I judging my spouse's motive?

6. Am I able to express my real emotional feelings to my spouse?

A Home Requires Upkeep and Repairs: Spend Time Together

It requires diligence to keep a home in good condition; it takes time. Spending quality time together expresses and refreshes the importance you feel for each other in your union.

Consider these statements about time:

Time: Spend time with your spouse, quality time, doing fun things like bird watching, photography, picnicking, taking a walk, sitting on the porch watching a sunset, building a brick border wall around a flower bed, or local antique shopping.

Illustration: *Going to Antique Shops*

My husband loved football and all kinds of sports, but I loved antique shops and any kind of treasure shop. He went antiquing with me, even though he did not particularly enjoy antique shopping. He went with me so we could spend some time together. He would just wander around at times, or if he found an old antique chair or couch, he would sit while I hunted for junk or treasures. He might have been bored, but he went anyway and learned to enjoy our time together. And every once in a while, he found something he wanted!

Time: Ecclesiastes 6:9: "What the eyes see is better than what the soul desires. This too is futility and striving after wind" (NASB).

- Find time for your mate. Do not waste time wanting something; it is like "striving after wind." Enjoy what you have and be thankful.
- Do not live in the past. Let it go and get on with life. It is never too late to get ahead. Do not talk, think, or meditate on the unenjoyable past history, but look to the future.
- Take the time to take care of the little things, and do not worry when those little things get big. Talk to God, talk it over with your mate, and trust God that you both can work it out. Catch little foxes. Remove hindrances.
  - Song of Solomon 2:15 – "Catch for us the foxes the little foxes that ruins the vineyards, our vineyards that are in bloom" (NIV).
- When your mate says, "I do not understand," take the time to say, "Tell me why," and then really listen.
- Locate things that hijack your time and get rid of them. Talk to each other and have a quality time of uninterrupted conversation.

- Question: "What will you sacrifice or give up for your mate?" Will he give up a one-day hunting trip? Will she give up a day with the girls? Give touches of affection in the morning, during the day, and at night.

Time: The question your mate may be asking in his or her heart, related to how much importance you place on time spent together, might be, "How much time do you have for me?" or "After the Lord, am I your top priority?"

- Pursue your spouse as if you have just met. Do not put other things first. After your relationship with the Lord, invest your time, energy, effort, and the pursuit of your mate as your top priority.
- Problems can be unreal, or they can have unrealistic expectations. List your top five problems and then work on solving them.

Illustration: *Personal Counseling*

The pastor Reverend Peter Lord's wife counseled me several times. One time in particular, she taught me that instead of leaving our problems, we needed to solve them. And so I knew that my husband and I needed to resolve some of our issues and be more involved with spending time together rather than spending time rehashing the same problems over and over again. We can let house upkeep, repairs, or other things go, but then we usually get stressed out because we know that if we tended to these things quickly, we could enjoy other things more. This principle applies to dealing with stress in a marriage. Stress can cause blood pressure problems and other health issues. Deal with marriage stress, and do not leave it unsolved, for it could very well show up later as larger, more serious problems.

Answer the following questions.

1. Do I plan and endeavor to spend time with my spouse? How often?

2. Do we spend quality time together? What do I need to give up or sacrifice for a better marriage? For singles: Are we spending quality time getting to know each other?

3. Is my spouse a top priority on my schedule? Does my work schedule take top priority? God first, spouse second, children third, work fourth. If God is first in total commitment, then all else will fall into place.

4. Discover the things that are hijacking your time together and plan to get rid of those interruptive issues.

5. Make investments of your time, energy, and effort in your spouse and pursue these as top priorities. Make a list of ways to spend time with your spouse.

Curb Appeal: Intentional Friendship in Marriage

A home should have an appealing and inviting environment. Couples should develop a real and transparent friendship with each other. Your spouse should be your best friend.

Friendship is built on being faithful. Proverbs 17:17 says, "A friend loves at all times" (NIV), and friends are available for each other. Friendship between a husband and wife should be intentional.

Develop a friendship with your spouse. Believe that your spouse is unique. This bonding should be developed during the dating time. Some miss this friendship because the physical gets in the way during the dating time.

Wife: Agree to the special call that a wife is a good cheerleader, practices respectful behavior, and displays a quiet spirit. She believes in her husband.

- 1 Peter 3:3-4 – "Your beauty should not come from outward adornment, such as elaborate hairstyles and the wearing of gold jewelry or fine clothes. Rather, it should be that of your inner self, the unfading beauty of a gentle and quiet spirit, which is of great worth in God's sight" (NIV).

Husband: Agree to the special call that a husband is a good provider of finances and security. He is a responsible leader and loves his wife as Christ loves the Church.

Friends embrace each other's differences. They become compatible in character and in values. Instead of tolerating your differences, you can celebrate your differences. Talk about your differences lovingly. Do not criticize your mate's differences in front of others. Friends usually have the same spiritual principles and values.

Illustration: *Mate Disagreements*

My husband and I had a huge disagreement on how the end-time events (when Christ comes back) would take place, what would happen first and what would happen next. This was a theological issue and not a spiritual or value issue. So, we could agree on the important day-by-day events and still have some belief differences. Some beliefs are important and should be decided before marriage, and some we can just accept. An issue like church denominational choice might be an issue to decide upon for unity in the marriage. But issues like the chronology of end-time events leave room for individual beliefs.

Be real and transparent. Be a safe mate in a safe place and do not be judgmental.

Go into each other's worlds; work hard at being fun. Friends have special fun times. Have weekly date trips or do special, inexpensive activities for an entire evening.

Bear each other's burdens. Friends serve one another. You may have times when you are hurting, but in a friendship, you always have someone there to help you during difficult times.

When spouses are also friends, they provide for the needs of each other in a marriage:

- Mates
- Conversations
- Openness and honesty
- Communication
- Affection
- Respect
- Security
- Friendship
- Loyalty

The gift of blessings can also bring the gift of burdens. Larger blessings equal bigger burdens. When God gives you larger blessings, it means God knows you can handle bigger burdens.

Answer the following questions.

1. Is my spouse or my spouse-to-be my best friend? Do we have a unique, one-of-a-kind relationship? Do we just tolerate each other?

2. Am I putting down or criticizing my spouse in front of others? If so, why? For singles: Am I beginning a pattern of putting down or criticizing my future mate? If so, why, and can I start a new pattern of admiration or honor?

3. Am I embracing our differences in a positive and loving way?
   - Friends are mates.
   - Friends have open conversations with honesty.
   - Friends communicate and respect each other.
   - Friends are loyal and guard their eyes.
   - Friends feel secure with each other.

4. What are we doing separately or together to build our friendship for a lifetime?

Communication with the Builder: Hear and Understand

Different types and levels of communication are used in building a home as well as in building a marriage. Both the husband and the wife should discover and learn to apply the highest quality and skills of communication with each other. Communication is a key factor in a beautiful and lasting relationship.

Three Types of Communication:

1. Reactive communication. A husband or wife reacts in anger to disagreements and problems. Reactive communication usually occurs after the fact.

2. Radioactive communication. This type of communication might include explosive or argumentative words, shouting, or yelling.

3. Proactive communication. The couple talks over the problems and disagreements and listens to each other. Proactive communication usually eliminates problems before they begin or before communication gets explosive. Proactive communication resolves issues in several ways:

- Spouses talk about the issues. Respect is when neither person tries to control the other. It is knowing each other's wants and needs.

- Spouses resolve the issues, even if they need help with counseling. When needed, they give each other space and time to think. What you think and feel is just as important as what the other person thinks and feels, so respect yourself.

- Go on a vision retreat. You will receive peace and blessings from a vision retreat. The purpose is to hear God's vision for your marriage. Pray, talk, discuss, and ask what God wants in your marriage.

- Communicate what is important. Good is the enemy of God's best. Make marginal investments. Invest extra time in God's word and in prayer. Limit activities to invest time with God. Invest in extra resources. Save money but spend or give to others. Invest in relationships. Spend time with others, as it is an opportunity to do God's work of ministry. Challenge: Plan for thinking time to set goals.

Illustration*: Friendship*

A couple was lonely when they moved to a new location. They invited a second couple over for dinner. The second couple introduced a third couple, and so on, until the group got to seven couples sharing a potluck or gathering to eat out. They became lifelong friends. They spent many years developing great communication skills with each other!

Encourage your spouse's strengths. Do not nag, yell, scream, use harsh words, or complain about his or her weaknesses; do not judge, criticize, resent, condemn, belittle, and do not try to remold him or her with your own hands. When your actions or words force your spouse to take a course of action, he or she may begin to withdraw in confusion or turn to more pleasant things. If it is a problem of one mate doing all the work and the other lazing around, then agree to a Honey Do List and make it fun, a competition, or a game. Husband and wife may need to get the "log of bad attitudes" out of their lives.

Three Illustrations: *Sharing the Load*

- *Both spouses work. They come home, she cooks dinner, and he helps with their child's homework and cleans up.*
- *Both spouses work. He loves to cook, so she helps with their child's homework and helps clean up.*
- *Both spouses work. One spouse sits and lets the other spouse do all the work—cooking, helping with homework, cleaning up—while he or she watches television.*

Everything should be "ours" in a marriage. A spouse hiding money or spending large amounts without mutual agreement causes resentment if he or she sneak around. Or it may cause fears, or a lack of trust, or a suspicious mind.

Encourage your spouse even when you do not feel like it. Do it anyway!

God is the Leader of your marriage. Let God be God and talk out problems and write down solutions. If you cannot come to a solution, then pray and ask God for help. The illustration of sweeping problems under the rug was shared previously, but it warrants a mention here.

Illustration: *Solving Problems*

My husband and I tended to sweep problems under the rug until it became so bumpy we could not walk on it. We began counseling and found a solution. The problem: dirty clothes anywhere but in the hamper. The solution: I designed a dirty clothes hamper, and my husband was happy to build—and to use—it.

Encourage your mate with these verbal expressions:

- "Go on ... I see."
- "How do you feel?"
- "Tell me about ..."

- Both should admit when you can: "I am sorry!"
- Use open questions (not closed).
- Use reflective responses.

Summarize: ("This is what I hear you saying"):
Communication is transmitting ideas and thoughts to another person who is able to receive and understand your message as intended. When a person understands the idea as intended, this enhances the relationship.

Illustration: *Working Toward a Solution*

A husband wanted his wife to take a certain action, but he only hinted at it. Every time they hit a certain subject related to the problem, anger flared up, and the other spouse responded in anger. This scenario was repeated over and over until they finally solved the problem.

Communication may be verbal or non-verbal. When the idea is understood, it should bring peace.

Illustration: *My Dad and Stepmom*

My dad and stepmom would sit side by side on the couch watching television, or they would be outdoors on a bench. From time to time, they would just look at each other and grin lovingly while holding hands, as if they were teenagers in love. Their non-verbal communication was beautiful to see!

One of the difficulties is making ourselves understood. It is possible for more than one message to be implied. People pick up on non-verbal communication.

At any time, there may be six or more possible messages:

- What do you mean to say? Sender's intent.
- What you actually said.
- What the other person hears you say.
- What the other person thinks he hears.
- What the other person says about what you said.
- What do you think the other person said about what you said, or what you think the other person meant in response?

What we meant is that we want the other person to hear and to understand us.

- Be an active listener. Be respectful and respond to feelings (not behavior).
- Communicate that you care and understand, or that you are trying to understand.
- Help the other person to talk it out.
- Help identify your emotions and your mate's emotions.
- Consider the following regarding active listening:
  - A roadblock is "no communication." The silent treatment does not work. However, a quiet, reserved,

and thinking-type personality may need more time to process his or her thoughts and, thus, is not communicating while he or she is in the process-thinking mode.

- o Do not suggest a premature solution before the other person is ready and in agreement.
- o Do not argue or establish the "facts."
- o Give permission when needed.
- o Listening requires consuming time. Be willing to sacrifice your time.

Five levels of communication:

1. Fantasy Level – Unreal
2. Factual Level – Facts, no personal input level
3. Fellowship Level – Ideas, judgments, and philosophy
4. Feeling Level – Willingness to discuss feelings
5. Freedom Level – Share dreams, ideas, intimacy (share innermost secrets, fears, failures with no fear of being rejected). To be completely known, accepted, and still be loved is the ideal true marriage.

A good resource for further study on communicating well with your spouse is *Communication: Key to Your Marriage* (Wright, 2012).

Answer the following questions.

1. Do we have long-range goals and a vision for communication in our marriage, or do we need counseling on how to communicate? Do we just need a retreat to help us resolve our issues and problems?

2. Is God the real leader in our marriage, or have we put God on the back burner?

3. What type of communicator am I? Reactive? Radioactive? Proactive?

4. Do we have good communication skills, or do we have roadblocks, such as:

    - The silent treatment
    - Arguing about facts or theories, or premature solutions
    - Slamming the door and leaving
    - Lack of listening or understanding

5. Communication can be verbal or nonverbal. Do my facial and body movements express respect and love? Does my nonverbal communication lack an emotional feeling of love?

6. Am I a great listener? Do I want to be the center of attention all the time?

7. What is my greatest need as a communicator in my marriage?

A House Becomes a Home: Soulmates

[This section will review the purpose of marriage.]

A house becomes a home when the homeowners move in and add their personal touches. In marriage, the couple adds their personal touch, gradually developing a strong oneness.

Myths about Soulmates:

1. *"My perfect soulmate will be just like me. We will always want to do the same things."*

   Truth: Soulmates may be very different. In fact, they are sometimes opposites.

2. *"If I marry my soulmate, we will not have problems. We will always agree. We will not have arguments."*

   Truth: All marriages will have problems. Couples have to work on solving their problems. Husband and wife work together, give and take, yield, surrender, and sometimes compromise. Some couples do not have huge disagreements; however, all couples still have problems to solve.

3. *"My soulmate will meet all my needs and make me happy all the time."*

Truth: Basic needs can only be met by God. Husbands and wives need to turn to God to make them happy, blessed, and joyful. Expecting your soulmate to make you happy is an unrealistic expectation.

Positives about Soulmates:

1. *Generous soul* – Give words and kindness to your soulmate. Give time and energy, give and sow into your marriage. Soulmates are not born; they are made.

   - Proverbs 11:25 – "A generous person will prosper; whoever refreshes others will be refreshed" (NIV).

2. *Priority* – God is first in a marriage, but the marriage is the top priority over children, activities, and anything else. After your relationship with God, the marriage relationship is next in priority. Give your life to esteem your mate.

3. *Empathy* – Be sensitive to how your soulmate feels. Be empathetic and sympathetic. Empathy is a choice. Let your will rule over your emotions. Sympathy is seeing things from your soulmate's point of view.

4. *Caring, Love, Chemistry, Empathy, Sensitive* – These are choices of AGAPE love. Agape love is a commitment. Commitment is a lifetime decision. Five minutes a day of empathetic listening can resurrect the dead.

Answer the following questions.

1. Are we responding to the Four Basic Needs in our
    marriage?

    -   Acceptance
    -   Identity
    -   Purpose
    -   Security

2. How much time do I spend with God? Do we spend time
    together reading the Bible, praying, or memorizing
    Scriptures?

3. Have I, or do I, believe any of these myths about
    marriage?

    -   "My soulmate will provide all my needs."
    -   "Sex is going to make our marriage great!"
    -   "We will never argue, we will not have problems, and
        we will always be happy."
    -   "We will be happy if we have this or that."

4. What in our marriage or marriage plans proves that we are
    soulmates? List these proofs.

5. What are some positives about being soulmates in a
    marriage?

6. Do I need to develop, or do I already have, a lifetime commitment goal of expressing agape love (God's love)?

Maintenance along the Way: Servanthood in Marriage

Just like maintenance on a house keeps things in order and running smoothly, having a servant's heart in a marriage creates a loving attitude and helps things run smoothly in the home.

The greatest attitude in marriage is "I am your servant," not "I am your slave."

Illustration: *Picking Up Clothes*

My husband had been a bachelor for a long time before we married. So, being a bachelor, he had a habit of just dropping his clothes on the floor or leaving a mess around the house. We were still newlyweds, and after a few days, I firmly said to him, "Honey, I can either be your slave and pick up and clean up after you, or I can be your wife. Which do you want?" From then on, he picked up after himself.

A spouse who has a servant attitude is secure in his or her marriage relationship. This attitude helps you meet your mate's needs and desires:

- Needs – A servant attitude creates a servant's heart.
- Desires – A servant attitude helps you to be a dream maker ("I am going to try to make your dreams come true.")

Servant's heart – A servant's heart helps create a deeper time of intimacy. Take turns serving each other. A servant spirit in marriage is a covenant seal. In marriage, sex is a covenant seal and a sign of sincere and forever commitment. Note: Some sensitive areas will need attention in a marriage at times:

- Stress or problems that are unresolved
- Communication bumps or needs
- Ignoring each other

A husband expresses his love through sex, and he needs sex. A wife can find fulfillment in sex; however, she needs the foreplay of intimate advances first. Plan time for intimate fun and enjoyment.

Plan a good time to communicate. Know the time that is good for both of you:

- Be romantic. Flowers, candy, or small love gifts can say, "You are on my heart," when things are in a tough or tight place.

Illustration: *Little Gifts*

As a symbol of romance, leave little wrapped candy kisses or notes around the house for your spouse to find. Say, "Sweetheart,

when you find a treasure around the house, it is an expression of
my love for you. When you find one, it means, 'I love you 100 times
more!'"

- Tell the truth in love. Sometimes, telling the truth may be needed, but timing is important. It is not a time to nag or to complain or to gripe; it is a time to be honest about your feelings or needs.
- Listen until your mate is calm and seems to not have any more to say.
- Do not raise your voice. Talk quietly, respect your spouse, and remain loving in your tone of voice.
- Spare the details when sharing a problem. Women love details, whereas men want the facts and not the details. When things are on edge, women should straighten out their emotions before expressing their feelings, and men should be aware of trying to get to the root of a problem when emotions are strong.
- Allow for reaction time. When the wife presents something, she should wait and let the husband either mull it over or start all over. And the same is true in reverse: the husband should allow the wife reaction time.

Have a discipline of praying together every day, even if it is for a short moment. Schedule praying over needs, problems, worries, or anything else. It is a wonderful opportunity to express love to God for your mate.

Defining moments – Stop fighting God:

- Disagreement times – Affirm what your mate said and agree that he or she has a right to be angry. James 1:19 states, "My dear brothers and sisters, take note of this: Everyone should be quick to listen, slow to speak and slow to become angry" (NIV). Repeat to your mate, "This is what I heard you say," in a loving, forgiving, compassionate way. Mirror your response and listen.

- Allow each other to dialogue—first, one spouse and then the other spouse.

- Do not lump 10 extra unrelated things in the argument, and do not bring up past history that has already been settled and forgiven. Consider these verses about love and how to rightfully handle anger:
  - 1 Corinthians 13:5 – "Love does not dishonor others, it is not self-seeking, it is not easily angered, it keeps no record of wrongs" (NIV).
  - Ephesians 4:26 – "In your anger do not sin: Do not let the sun go down while you are still angry" (NIV).

- Train in non-defensive responses. Do not escalate the problem by becoming defensive. Your spouse does not want to hear your defenses. What he or she wants is for you to understand why you hurt, offended, or angered him or her. Your spouse is angry with you. It is possible that the offended party may have misread or made untrue assumptions. You have to be sensitive to the problem and the needs of your spouse. So during these times, try to be extremely understanding and try not to make assumptions; check to see if you have misread a situation.

Defensive actions may say to some spouses, "I have not offended and here is why ..." Wait to share your defenses, explanations, or reasons when you have been wrongly judged at a later, less volatile time.

Illustration: *Person Offended*

A person I was in contact with many times was continually offended because she always assumed she knew the reasons for my actions, rather than trying to find out the truth of my real motivations. When I tried to tell her that her assumptions were wrong, and if I tried to explain and defend my actions, she would cut me off in anger and say that I could not defend myself. She told me the only reason I was defending myself was that I was trying to get out of my guilt and say that I was not guilty.

When we are offended and we let others know, we should listen to their side of the situation instead of assuming we know it all.

Answer the following questions.

1. Do I have a servant's attitude? What am I doing or saying that says I am a servant? What am I doing or saying that says I do not have a servant's heart?

2. If I do not have a servant's heart, what actions do I need to add or take away to be a better example of a servant?

3. A servant spirit in a marriage is a covenant seal. What are some of the stressful areas that are hindrances to our covenant seal?

4. Do I know what my spouse or future spouse needs (love, understanding, time to think, a hug)?

5. Am I a good listener? Am I truthful with my spouse? Am I willing to let my spouse be right on a particular issue?

6. Am I able to use non-defensive responses to problem areas, and am I willing to accept blame for some areas? (It is not what happens to you but what happens inside you and how you respond.)

Enhancement Ideas: Beautify Your Marriage

Houses may need to be refurbished or remodeled along the way.
All marriages need extra attention at times.

Consider these ideas for beautifying, embellishing, and adorning your marriage:

1. Use candles for every meal or for special meals.

2. List many reasons for saying, "I love you," and put these in a decorated jar to read in special moments.

3. Repeat your wedding vows on your anniversary or at times when you both need to hear them.

4. Sometimes, you need to set the atmosphere for quality time. To help return the loving atmosphere, for the next 28 days, try these things to increase your communication.

   - Talk to each other. Schedule quality time for an uninterrupted conversation.

   - Do some type of activity together, like take a walk, sit on the porch and watch the sunset, or build a brick

border wall around a flower bed. Some of these
activities can include the children.

- Give touches of affection in the morning, during the
  day, and at night.

Do some type of kindness deed for your mate: foot
massage, back rub, manicure or pedicure, or fix an extra-
special favorite meal.

Say loving words to your spouse or write loving notes and
leave them around the house. Use clippings, photos,
humorous stories, and other things to make a poster or
collage thanking your spouse for being a hard worker or a
good provider.

5. Put glow-in-the-dark letters and stars on the ceiling for a
   message of love.
6. Create a special basket decorated for the TV remote
   control.
7. Cut out romantic messages from newspapers and
   magazines. Put them in a letter and send it to your mate.
8. Spend time together. Do things together.

Illustration: *Make a List*

*A couple should brainstorm and create a list of things they
would love to do together in their lifetime—interesting places to
travel to, activities to complete, new things to learn, hobbies to*

pursue ... the list can include anything the couple would love to accomplish together.

Answer the following questions.

1. Do we repeat or celebrate our wedding vows in some special way on our anniversary or at other times? Do we buy some sweet type of memento for our special day to remember that particular anniversary?

2. How can I enhance, embellish, or adorn my marriage to make it more beautiful? List 50 ways. Try some of these ways on a regular basis.

Necessary Remodeling: From Unfaithfulness to Reconciliation

At times, a house requires necessary remodeling to make it more functional. When a mate has been unfaithful and wants to try reconciliation, consider these marriage "remodeling" ideas.

1. One thing the faithful mate can do to help is to ask questions:
   - Has the mate been unfaithful many times and wants to return each time?
   - Has the mate been unfaithful only once or twice?

2. Ask another set of questions:
   - Have I been through this many times before, and there is no repentance?
   - Do I really love my spouse?
   - Am I doing my part in making our marriage great?
   - Am I willing to forgive?
   - Once forgiven, will I trust my spouse again?

3. The process of healing:

- The unfaithful mate seriously asks for forgiveness.

Illustration: *Nonchalant Attitude*

A preacher had an adulterous affair with a woman in his church. When he wanted to give up the affair and get back with his wife, he asked her to forgive him; however, he had such a nonchalant attitude as if it was nothing. There was not even a hint of repentance; just the monotone words, "Will you forgive me?" She could not sense a regretful spirit in him, and she was deeply hurt by his unemotional attitude. Needless to say, they did not get back together.

- The faithful mate **sincerely forgives and verbally gives a confirmation of forgiveness**. The faithful mate NEVER mentions it again. NEVER! There is never even a hint of alluding to the sin. Ever.
- The faithful mate **prays** for the unfaithful mate to become stronger in the area of fidelity and seeks ways to strengthen that weakness. Pray for the real changes that are needed.
- The faithful mate **asks himself/herself questions**:
  - What weaknesses or failures in my life may have contributed to the unfaithful mate's infidelity?
  - What areas of my life do I need to strengthen?

You build your marriage by removing destructive elements in yourself first.

- The faithful mate does not accuse, is not suspicious, and does not quiz his or her mate in that area of sexual weakness.
- The faithful mate finds ways to encourage, exhort, praise, complement, and uplift the unfaithful mate. Admire, esteem, and find your mate's potential strengths and work on those.
- Both mates seek to communicate more deeply and seek healing on both sides.
- Both mates pray together and read Scripture, memorize, and meditate on the Word of God.
- The unfaithful mate determines to never let it happen again.
- The unfaithful mate asks for prayer when he or she feels weak or has temptations. Seek a friend, pastor, or counselor to pray with you, or have your mate pray with you.
- The unfaithful mate should try to focus on meeting the needs or desires of his or her mate and figure out how to strengthen his or her own marriage.

- The unfaithful mate needs to discover how deeply he or she has hurt his or her mate (and their children). Unfaithfulness in many areas leaves soul wounds.

Illustration: *Frank and Bunny Constantino*

Frank Costantino was a professional criminal, and he was sent to prison. He had a personal encounter with Christ and got saved in the office of Chaplain Max Jones. After his release from prison, he began a prison ministry. When he came home from prison, he did not realize how deeply he had wounded his wife, Bunny. In his book, more than a Miracle: The Ministry of Aftercare, he said, "In many ways, I had deeply hurt Bunny. Some wounds are so deep that the mind will not focus on them. These are the wounds of the spirit. ... What could heal these? Time alone does not heal them. I had to show Bunny that indeed I had changed, that I cared about her and would not hurt her again. With God's help through prayer, this really worked. Our marriage was well on its way to total recovery" (1985, p. 26).

However, some people keep those wounds for a lifetime and never heal.

Illustration: *Divorced Couple*

A couple had some major problems in their marriage. She left him and went to another town for a job, still married to him. She started living with another man, unbeknownst to her husband. She eventually divorced her husband, and he was devastated when he found out that she had dated and lived with another man while they were still married. This deeply wounded former husband is still angry, bitter, and resentful. He is not willing to deal with his hurts and keeps them inside, so he is unable to get the healing he needs.

4. The unfaithful mate tries, with God's help, to …

- **Bring restoration** to all family members affected by his or her past actions.
- **Reconcile anything** that needs mending, healing, or "loving glue." We have considered the following illustration previously, but let's review it again with a view toward oneness in a marriage after restoration and reconciliation.

Illustration: *Glued Together*

Glue two pieces of paper together, allow the glue to dry completely, and then try to separate the two pieces of paper. What might happen to the two pieces of paper? … But consider these verses:

We "can do all things through Him who strengthens" us (Philippians 4:13, NASB).

- *"Put on love, which is the perfect bond of unity" (Colossians 3:14, NASB).*

- *"Love is patient, love is kind. ... Love never fails" (1 Corinthians 13:4a, 8a, NIV).*
- **Make restitution.** Ask God for creative ways to make restitution and bring about restoration.
- **Build a new relationship** with all affected family members and work on deep Christian love and trust.
- **Have faith that God will restore everything and receive hope** for the future. When there is no faith, ask God for restored faith.
  - Philippians 2:13 – "… it is God who works in you to will and to act in order to fulfill his good purpose" (NIV).
  - **Build up the marriage** by removing broken, warped, cracked, damaged, and misshapen bricks. If the damaged bricks are not removed and replaced with strong bricks, it creates a weakness in the foundation of your marriage, and problems, troubles, and trials will get bigger, like a damaged house foundation.
    - James 1:19-20 – "My dear brothers and sisters, take note of this: Everyone should be quick to listen, slow to speak and slow to become angry, because human anger does not produce the righteousness that God desires" (NIV).

- James 4:7-8, 10 – "Submit yourselves, then, to God. Resist the devil, and he will flee from you. Come near to God and he will come near to you. Wash your hands, you sinners, and purify your hearts, you double-minded. … Humble yourselves before the Lord, and he will lift you up" (NIV).
- Repair the damaged heart and fill it with love. This must be done with God's help.
- Build by expressing outward loving actions. Love is a verb.
  - Praise and approval
  - Fulfilling needs
  - A wife submitting to her husband's leadership
  - Adapting to and serving your mate
  - Obey, submit, and change
  - A husband loving his wife as Christ loves the Church.

It is agape love—not feelings, impulse, or natural inclinations. It is a deep commitment that gives sacrificially, even in adverse circumstances. Love is an unconditional acceptance of an imperfect person.

Answer the following questions.

1. If one mate has been unfaithful or is tempted to be unfaithful because of past failures, what steps will we take to heal our marriage?

2. If I have been the unfaithful mate in the past, have I sincerely repented and asked for forgiveness? Am I willing to be a faithful, anointed mate for the rest of my life? What steps have I taken to heal the soul wounds I have caused in others? In my family?

3. If my spouse has been the unfaithful mate in the past, how willing am I to forgive and try to help the healing process on both our parts? Am I full of anger, bitterness, and resentment for my spouse's past failure or failures? Am I willing to start all over with total forgiveness and rebuild our marriage? Am I willing to heal and never mention the sin of failure?

Soul Wounds

Consider these questions: Am I willing to pray until my soul wounds are totally healed? Am I willing to forgive, pray, and receive godly ministering help for me to heal? It may take time.

- Psalm 31:14-16 – "But I trust in you, Lord; I say, 'You are my God.' My times are in your hands; deliver me from the hands of my enemies, from those who pursue me. Let your face shine on your servant; save me in your unfailing love" (NIV).

- Jeremiah 31:3 – "The Lord appeared to us in the past, saying: 'I have loved you with an everlasting love; I have drawn you with unfailing kindness'" (NIV).

- Deuteronomy 31:8 – "The Lord himself goes before you and will be with you; he will never leave you nor forsake you. Do not be afraid; do not be discouraged" (NIV).

- Psalm 73:23 – "Yet I am always with you; you hold me by my right hand" (NIV).

God's counsel equals guidance.

In his devotional book, *hope for Each Day: Words of Wisdom and Faith*, Billy Graham says, "Affliction can be a means of refining and of purification. ... So our lives must sometimes pass through God's furnace of affliction before they can bring forth something beautiful and useful to Him" (2006, p. 105).

Many events can be afflictions that leave us alone and single, such as the death of a spouse, separation, betrayal, unfaithfulness, or divorce. Any of these trials or crises can be a furnace in our lives.

According to some authors, the four basic personalities include the following: The Sanguine, the Melancholic, the Choleric, and the Phlegmatic (Childs, 1995; LaHaye, 1994; Littauer, 2000). People fall under one of these or a combination of two or more. For some, the trials they face that leave them single ultimately become furnaces in their lives, and for others, they may go through transforming personality changes.

In this section, this change will be referred to as "persona" so as not to confuse it with the four personalities mentioned above. A person can still have the same personality, but the change can be so strong, because of soul wounds, that he or she develop a different persona. Sometimes this persona becomes negative or unfavorable and can even be detrimental to the hurting person. Some people become negative so that they do not have to deal with the situations.

In this section, these afflictions will be referred to as "soul wounds" or "personality changes" because these trials may affect people deeply in their souls.

The Divorce Wound

Divorce is such a gargantuan topic. Even though this study is about making marriage wonderful, it would be remiss not to briefly mention some observations concerning the subject of divorce that may help someone to heal and have a healthier marriage.

Divorce leaves some people with deep feelings of rejection, hurt, disappointment, and perhaps even distrust of others. For these deeply wounded souls, some turn to God, and some turn to alternate things such as alcohol, drugs, sexual misbehavior, or deviant lifestyles to ease the pain. Some turn away from God, asking, "God, why did You not save me from these deep emotional hurts?" or "Why did You not answer my prayers?" and so on.

Some turn to God and become healed, turning their lives around. However, some hold onto the anguish, pretending they are just fine. Those who hold the hurt inside may deny the truth and tell themselves that the pain is not there anymore. They live in a state of denial.

If a person has been divorced more than once, then the repercussions can go deeper into the psyche, the heart or the soul of their being. Their reactions to life and to others can take many forms. So, instead of personality, the term persona—a part of a person seen by others and played out in that person's life—is being used. This list is not complete, but several identified and observed persona characteristics are listed here:

1. **The Closed-off Persona:** This persona usually finds meaning in other things, such as sports, recreation, fishing, hunting, crocheting, knitting, or painting. The closed-off persona has a few support people. This persona responds inside with, "I will not let you in my life because I do not trust you nor anyone," or "I will not let you into my life because I do not want any more wounds, especially no deep suffering," or "I will entertain and make people laugh so they cannot know me nor the depth of my problems, hurts, and struggles."

2. **The Reclusive Persona:** This persona has an attitude of "life never changes." Therefore, they think, "Since material things or junk do not hurt me, I can collect those lovable possessions." Likely inside, this persona is saying, "I will not discuss anything personal with you nor anyone else. That way, I do not have to open up and share my past anguish. I can just push these hurts aside and pretend the misery is not here anymore." The reclusive persona has an extremely small

support group, if any. Also, this persona may take many avenues, for example:

- Becomes a recluse in all of life.
- Sinks into a deep depression (does not open blinds or curtains, does not do normal duties, does not take care of things, becomes a junk collector).
- Avoids conflicts at all costs.
- Ignores problems, saying, "It will all work out."
- Has no real purpose or goals in life; becomes a television addict or a couch potato.
- Gains weight due to emotional eating.
- Takes on a fatalistic attitude.
- Never gets close to anyone, not even family members.
- Becomes deeply introverted and does not ask others about their problems. If this persona does ask, it is usually out of politeness and not out of genuine concern. The reclusive persona will let others share the depth of their hurts, but this persona cannot share their own needs. They pretend that they do not need anything.

3. **The Controlling Persona:** This persona feels like they have lost control of their life. Thus, this persona's deep hurts become a chance to hurt others by controlling them. Sometimes, the controlling persona's character takes on a persona different from their real personality, for example:

- This persona tries to control their children, their new or former spouse, their friends' and family's lives, and their own life.

- The controlling persona tries to control others by manipulating them so they can torment others in the same way they have suffered in the past.

- This persona is jealous of the wonderful things that happen to couples in a good marriage.

- The controlling persona usually has not dug deeply into the woundedness of their own heart to experience and receive healing; thus, this persona sees the pain of their own experiences and does not or cannot see their own faults. However, most people with a controlling persona can see the faults of others quickly and become easily offended at the slightest irritation.

- This persona makes a lot of assumptions and judgments as to why others do things. Usually, these assumptions are wrong because the controlling persona assumes that the motive of the behavior is, "You did this to hurt me!" or "You did this because you want to control me!" or "You did this because you are mean!" or "You did this because you want to reject me!" The controlling persona can feel that the rejection happens "little by little" because the other person is trying to gnaw away at them. Usually, this persona has a very small supportive group that really does not know them. This persona looks for a support person who agrees with their assumed motives, and the controlling persona's support friends are usually social acquaintances.

- o 1 Corinthians 13:5 – "Love does not dishonor others, it is not self-seeking, it is not easily angered, it keeps no record of wrongs" (NIV).

Illustration: *"My Next Wife"*

A husband was angry about his divorce and said, "I want my next wife to be meek, gentle, and quiet." By this, he meant, "I want to be the dominate person in our marriage."

4. **The Perfect (or Not-My-Fault) Persona:** This persona may have some deep-seated feelings of "I am right!" or "My way is the right way to do things."
   - The perfect persona may have feelings of, "My way is the best way, so do not tell me about your plans."
   - This persona may have deep feelings of being rejected or hurt when they did everything possible to save their marriage, but it failed anyway. "I did all that I could do to save things, but it dissolved no matter what I did." The offending mate is 110% wrong and sinful, but this rejected perfect persona may be only 10% wrong, so they say, "It was not my fault!" This perfect persona

mate has chosen to put themselves above God, above truth, above right, and above the needs in their marriage. A marriage break-up is never one person's fault; plenty of blame exists for both sides. However, the percentage of right and wrong may be different. The perfect persona is usually looking at the divorce or separation from their own self-centered perspective. Usually, fault occurs on both sides; but usually, God speaks to the rejected or hurt person who is less wrong because that person is the one listening to God. What the hurt person wants to say is, "God, why do you not talk to my mate? He or she is the one who did wrong and deserted me."

- The perfect persona is usually the victim in the divorce or separation. They were the ones doing everything to salvage things for the most part, but they were deserted anyway because of their mate's sins and not their own sins or failures. Usually, the support group for this persona has had the same things happen to them, and they take sides in the separation.

  o Habakkuk 1:2-3 – "How long, Lord, must I call for help, but you do not listen? Or cry out to you, 'Violence!' but you do not save? Why do you make me look at injustice? Why do you tolerate wrongdoing? Destruction and violence are before me; there is strife, and conflict abounds" (NIV).

- The perfect persona uses a lot of defense mechanisms and blames others.

5. **The Rebellious, Bitter, and Angry Persona**: Usually, this persona is aware of the problems and changes in their marriage, but he or she is an innocent, unsuspecting, or even a naïve person. Things get worse, and the angry persona still does not see the tell-tale signs of the looming separation nor the oncoming divorce papers.

- When the unfaithful mate asks for a divorce or tells their spouse they are leaving the house, the faithful person feels devastated and emotionally crippled in their soul and emotions.
- Usually, the unfaithful mate has been cheating for quite some time, and in addition, has chosen a new mate. Many times, the new mate does not measure up to the unsuspecting spouse in several ways, maybe in looks, weight, morals, racial difference, or maybe the new mate has a totally different character type.
- Because of the rejection, when the separation is long past or the divorce is final, many times the angry persona feels

so deeply hurt that they become angry, upset, and bitter with feelings of inner rebellion. These feelings can become so strong that the angry persona feels they can never trust anyone again. Many times, they become a negative persona when their personality has been joyful, or at least positive, previously.

- If this bitter, angry, and hurt persona does not get help or get healed, sometimes the depth of this wound can cause isolation.

- Sometimes, they become critical and negative.

- Sometimes, they become a controlling persona, too.

- Some become overly sensitive and are offended by the slightest thing. In fact, sometimes, the angry persona tends to look for and find things they see as offensive that are normally not offensive.

- Thus, many in this category become angrier, bitter, and resentful. Usually, they have an extremely small support group who have the same offended, negative attitude, or they reject anyone trying to support and help them.

  o Proverbs 29:11 – "Fools give full vent to their rage, but the wise bring calm in the end" (NIV).

  - This persona sometimes feels unloved by anyone, and it is hard to convince them that they are loved. They do not listen to the words, but they want actions that prove to them they are loved. Many times, the angry persona has been hurt by past family actions, more than one divorce, or separations, and they are not convinced that anyone loves them.

6. **The Relief Persona:** After an especially difficult marriage involving abuse of whatever type, parting ways may be necessary, even healthy, for both individuals. The happiness of this freedom could be intoxicating, allowing the relief persona to reach out in various ways.

   - After divorce, the relief persona may become narcissistic, have an inflated sense of importance, have a deep need for excessive attention and admiration, show a lack of empathy for others, or have further troubled relationships.
   - Divorce can bring remorse, depression, or heavy regret.
   - Divorce can also bring stretched financial situations, hardships, gossip, guilt, shame, suicidal thoughts, or even homelessness, depending upon a person's employability.

The Other-Than-Divorce Wound

Then, there is the person who lost their spouse to death or to total separation but is not a divorced persona.

7. **The Lost Reality Persona:** This persona has usually lost their spouse of 50+ years. Usually, they have been totally dependent on their mate and have spent all their lives together without much interaction with other couples, or they have not developed their own hobbies, interests, or outside world.

    - The lost reality persona's support system is usually based on the friends of the deceased spouse, and they do not have their own friends.

    - Much of the time, this persona holds on to the deceased person's personal belongings for months or even years.

Illustration: *Holding On*

When the surviving spouse does not move or remove anything that belonged to the deceased spouse (clothing, makeup, tools, work boots), it can be a problem for the lost reality persona.

- This persona loses touch with reality and may choose to start drinking or indulge in some other habit that is not good for them.

- Sometimes, the lost reality persona turns to affairs that cover up the healthy choice of looking at what has happened to them. Sometimes, they have mental and emotional trauma.

Illustration: *Losing Touch with Reality*

A man who drank lost touch with reality and left everything in the house just as it was. He refused to get rid of his wife's antiques. The next woman in his life said, "Everything in the house says his first wife is still here, and he will not get rid of anything of hers. I cannot live with that." They lived together for a while in his house, but things never changed, so she left.

These soul wounds are sometimes never healed because the deeply hurt person will not admit the depth of their wounds nor seek God to remove the problems. They need God to do a work of deep healing in their lives. Instead of choosing the right path, they tend to allow only surface healing and, thus, are unable to ever fully get back to normal. Due to the patch-up job, they tend to get offended repeatedly over issues in second or third marriages. They use several methods to cover up future difficulties:

- They withdraw more.
- They become argumentative.
- They try to control others or manipulate them.
- They see the patch-up job as permanent and complete when, at best, it is only a temporary fix.

These are only a few of the severe soul wounds, and for some, it is a case of various levels of these personas. Or it may be a combination of two or more. No one follows any of these exactly, and as previously indicated, there may be many more personas.

How to Heal from Soul Wounds

So the question is this: "How can I become healed of my deep soul wounds?"

God can heal any and all deep soul wounds. Here are some suggestions for receiving renewed life and healing.

1. Step One: Recognize that you are deeply, deeply wounded. Many people have been hurt for years and perhaps have stored up several offenses or denied them, or have buried those terrible problems under the rug. When someone suggests to them how to remove these inner feelings of hurt, they just shut down and do not want to deal with the depth of their injuries. So, Step One is to admit the unpleasantness of the depth of anger, bitterness, or resentment.

   - Psalm 103:3-5 – "The Lord forgives all your sins and heals all your diseases, he redeems your life from the pit and crowns you with love and compassion, and he satisfies your desires with good things so that your youth is renewed like the eagles" (NIV).
   - Ephesians 4:30-31 – "And do not grieve the Holy Spirit of God, with whom you were sealed for the day of

redemption. Get rid of all bitterness, rage and anger, brawling and slander, along with every form of malice" (NIV).

- Matthew 6:12 – "And forgive us our debts, as we also have forgiven our debtors" (NIV).

- James 5:16 – "Therefore confess your sins to each other and pray for each other so that you may be healed. The prayer of a righteous person is powerful and effective" (NIV).

2. Step Two: Believe that you can be healed. Know that you are in a battle. It is like you are rebuilding a wrecked ship.

3. Step Three: Believe that God can and will restore your broken spirit if you will release it to Him.

- Psalm 51:12, 14, 17 – "Restore to me the joy of your salvation and grant me a willing spirit, to sustain me. … Deliver me from the guilt of bloodshed, O God, you who are God my Savior, and my tongue will sing of your righteousness. … My sacrifice, O God, is a broken spirit; a broken and contrite heart you, God, will not despise" (NIV).

Because God has blessed us with the ability to think, choose, and imagine, sometimes we tend to think about the negative words and events from the past. In other words, what we have sincerely given to God at one point in time, we may take back many times and allow it to control our minds.

Recognize your anger, admit you have a wounded soul, and ask God to forgive your anger, resentments, bitterness, or bad attitudes. Release it all to Him. In other words, throw all of your excess baggage overboard. Set your priorities and decide what is important for your marriage.

4. Step Four: Give these deep hurts to God, even if you have done it a thousand times before. Only this time, take a new approach and make a list of the offenses. Tell God and admit the depth of every single awful and unpleasant thing that has happened to you. Tell God how much it hurts. Describe in detail the misery and agony of that particular situation.

    *   Psalm 54:2 – "Hear my prayer, O God; listen to the words of my mouth" (NIV).
    *   Psalm 55:22 – "Cast your cares on the Lord and he will sustain you, he will never let the righteous be shaken" (NIV).
    *   Psalm 62:8 – "Trust in him at all times, you people; pour out your hearts to him, for God is our refuge" (NIV).

Then, declare your forgiveness to that person (the one with the vile, aggressive, or revolting behavior) who offended you. Do not let go of God until you have felt and accepted His grace and His peace covering. Forgive, even if the person is deceased, has moved away, or you know you will never see them again. Many times, the offending party will never ask for your forgiveness. Sometimes, the offenses are very hurtful mentally or emotionally rather than physically. Recognize, specifically, how you have been abused. If you need to forgive someone who wronged you, tell God, "This hurts, but I forgive them," and ask Him to help you forgive the person who offended you. Put their name on the list. Read the list and then express to God that you have truly forgiven them.

5. Step Five: Take the list of hurts and either tear it up into tiny pieces or burn it as a visual so you know you have been cleared forever in your soul, conscience, and spirit. Cut the ropes of divorce and do not abandon the ship. Nothing changes God's purpose for your life. Commit to your marriage covenant. Remember, God is with you during every trial.

- Hebrews 13:5b – "Never will I leave you; never will I forsake you" (NIV).

The Comforter will give you peace–peace that the world cannot see nor understand. He gives us peace in the middle of our circumstances. Our total surrender brings treasures of peace and a new commitment. Some of our greatest treasures come from pain. God's love never leaves us. What can a person do if the mate is living with someone else or has remarried?

6. Step Six: Seek the mind of Christ. Another blessing God has given us is called "the mind of Christ." You are probably ready to seek His mind diligently. It is not an easy task, as we are fighting against God's enemy for our minds.

    - John 10:10 – "The thief comes only to steal and kill and destroy; I have come that they may have life, and have it to the full" (NIV).
        o   Satan's purpose is to steal, kill, and destroy.
        o   God's purpose is to give us an abundance of who Jesus is and give us His mind.

You may have fought this skirmish of hurts and forgiveness (the same ones) many times and in many ways, and you may have done battle over the same things over and over before; however, Satan wants to control you. His plan is to steal you away from Jesus; to kill you with wrong thoughts; and to gain strongholds in your life to destroy you, your mate's life, and your children's lives. He will use your past, present, and future to pull you away. He will use any deceitful device to destroy you. But God is on your side, and through Him, you can receive renewed life and healing.

Guidelines for Developing the Mind of Christ

Here are some guidelines for developing the Mind of Christ:

1. Realize there is a battle. Be willing to work.
2. Be willing, with the Lord's help, to continue working on soul-wounded healing. Think of yourself as a soldier.
3. Think about these things: You can *want*, you can *desire*, and you can *say the words*, "I choose a Christ-like mind." You can even *commit* yourself, but until you *obey* the Scriptures, you are not there. The battle begins. In Psalm 32:8, God says, "I will instruct you and teach you in the way you should go; I will counsel you with my loving eye on you" (NIV). You have to want a renewed mind, and then ask, "What is a renewed mind?" Remember, you have torn up or burned those old offenses, so you have a clear conscience.
4. Romans 12:1-2 gives you instructions on having a renewed mind:

"Therefore, I urge you, brothers and sisters, in view of God's mercy, to offer your bodies as a living sacrifice, holy and pleasing to God—this is your true and proper worship. Do not conform to the pattern of this world, but be transformed by the renewing of your mind. Then you will be able to test and approve what God's will is—his good, pleasing and perfect will" (NIV).

- Present your whole body, mind, will, and emotions to the Lord. Make this a ceremony of dedication you will remember for the rest of your life. It is between you and God. Present yourself as a living sacrifice, like in the Old Testament, where people brought lambs for their sacrifices. The lambs had to be without blemish when they were presented to God. You can present yourself to God as unblemished because you have cleared your conscience and spirit with everyone and with the Lord. Of course, after this special dedication of your life, you will still need to recommit yourself daily to the Lord. But this ceremony should begin a new habit of renewing your mind on a daily basis.

- After the dedication of your entire body, mind, will, and emotions, and giving your old thoughts to God and asking for His help, you can begin a new adventurous journey of scriptural mind renewal.

- Memorize and meditate on Scripture with a new mind. Go at your own pace. A suggestion is to memorize one Scripture per month, saying it over and over until you have it in your mind forever. You express your love to God through obedience.

- Be determined to live a changed life, putting God first in all you do. Like repairing an old house that needs remodeling, set your goal to restore and repair every area of your marriage with God's help.

- Ecclesiastes 3:14-15 – "I know that everything God does will endure forever; nothing can be added to it and nothing taken from it. God does it so that people will fear him. Whatever has already been, and what will be has been before, and God will call the past to account" (NIV).

- Ecclesiastes 4:9-12 – "Two are better than one, because they have a good return for their labor: If either of them falls down, one can help the other up. But pity anyone who falls and has no one to help them up. Also, if two lie down together, they will keep warm. But how can one keep warm alone? Though one may be overpowered, two can defend themselves. A cord of three strands is not quickly broken" (NIV). (The cord of three strands is the Lord, you, and your spouse.)

- Ecclesiastes 3:1, 11 – "There is a time for everything, and a season for every activity under the heavens. ... He has made everything beautiful in its time. He has also set eternity in the human heart; yet no one can fathom what God has done from beginning to end" (NIV).

- o Give thanks, praising and worshipping God for His work in building and repairing your former life and your marriage.

5. If these offenses are removed in your life now, in your marriage, or in your responses to your mate, find creative ways to overcome the areas that need repairing. For example:

- Explain or defend your actions when they seem offensive to your spouse. Say, "I could be wrong," or "Let me see if I can understand your side," or whatever it takes to clear things.

- Write notes or cards to let your spouse know he or she is loved or express your love in a visual way.

- Pray for blessings, gifts, and favors from God and others for your spouse.

- Pray for the armor of God to cover your family members as well as yourself.

- Pray for open ears to hear the Holy Spirit for heart healing and be filled with all kinds of creative ideas, thoughts, and precious ways to build and edify your spouse. Consider different ways to have fun with your spouse.

Answer the following questions.

1. Do I recognize one or more of the persona identities in my life as a result of past failures, an unfaithful mate, my spouse leaving me, or the death of my spouse?

2. Am I willing to go through the suggestions for soul wound healing? How and when will I plan to implement this endeavor?

3. Am I ready and motivated to use the guidelines for developing the mind of Christ in my marriage? What is my plan for my life with a renewed mind?

4. Do I need someone to counsel me in this discipleship program for my life? If so, who?

5. I realize that all of this takes time, effort, discipline, and patience. This whole program is a LIFE CHANGE. Am I committed to taking the steps to rebuild my marriage, just as a builder uses architectural plans to take the appropriate steps to build a home? Am I committed to the work of ongoing upkeep for my marriage, just as homeowners are committed to providing ongoing upkeep for their house?

After Completing This Section on Soul Wounds

Now that you have completed studying and researching some of the Lord's biblical principles for marriage, it is time to consider how you can put this learning into practical application in your marriage. Pray for the Lord's help and guidance, and then write out a plan and make a commitment, with the Lord's help, to build a stronger marriage. What steps will you and your spouse take to build a godly marriage?

Conclusion

The purpose and goal of this manual is to help couples—preparing for marriage or already married—to realize that with continuous and intentional effort, the steadfast application of God's principles, and His ongoing help, their marriages will be a picture of Christ and His bride, the Church.

It is my desire that comparing the steps in building a sturdy house with the steps in building a godly marriage will give you a mental, and perhaps a visual, picture of the *work* it takes to build an architectural structure, as well as the *work* it takes to build a strong and beautiful marriage. I pray that each couple will spend the necessary time and effort to develop and strengthen their oneness together.

And it is my hope that each couple will allow God's biblical principles to lead and guide their lives into a stronger and deeper marriage union, into a godly marriage built on the truth of the Word of God.

Appendix A: Uneven Spiritual Growth in Marriage

Land may sink or develop foundation problems. In building a marriage, soul wounds must be addressed.

1. Uneven Spiritual Growth – When one marriage mate has not grown spiritually as much as the other, the spiritual growth in the marriage is at an uneven level. Sometimes this creates problems. Perhaps the marriage began in one of these ways:

    -   The marriage started on a physical basis rather than on a friendship or spiritual level. Maybe the couple had sex before marriage and were not where they should have been spiritually.

    -   One spouse was a Christian, but not where he or she should have been with the Lord; one pretended to be a Christian, and the actual Christian was deceived.

Illustration: *A Deceitful Man*

A divorced man who was not a Christian started dating a Christian lady, and they attended church together. She thought he was honest and was a Christian. Not long after they started dating, he proposed to her on the church steps to emphasize and enhance his position. They had only dated for three months, so when he pretended to be a Christian in order to marry her, she was totally deceived and fooled. A Christian friend of hers suggested that the lady wait until she knew him better, but she was so enamored with his romantic gestures that she did not wait. And of course, they got married. After being married for only a few months, she realized she had been fooled and that he was a "womanizer." She worked extremely hard for several years to save their marriage, but he wanted to be free and asked for a divorce, which she gave him.

- Maybe both were faithful to begin with and were going to church, but the church split or had other problems and the weaker mate was affected by a lack of love in the church members.
- One mate might have been unfaithful to his or her spouse, or maybe both were unfaithful.
- One mate got involved with sinful actions that created a wall between them.

Illustration: *The Sin of Pornography*

Sometimes, mates do not inform each other of the sinful habits in which they engage. A husband and wife were having serious difficulties, and finally, he shared with her that he had a habit of viewing pornography. His struggle with pornography was affecting their marriage. She helped him, and finally, he broke the habit. They are both growing strong in their marriage and Christian walk now. It took time for him to overcome, but she was willing to see him through, and their marriage began to produce some wonderful testimonies as to God's help and healing. It took courage on the husband's part to confess his sin, and it took complete love and devotion on the wife's part to forgive her husband and to trust God to guide them.

Solving the Problem of Spiritual Growth vs. Non-Growth – Here are some suggested avenues for healing. This usually requires action on the part of the mate who is growing.

- Seek the Lord's guidance, His help, and His strength.
- Be doubly willing to submit and change even though you are only 10% wrong, and your mate is 110% wrong. Often, we hear, "Why do I always have to apologize when he or she is the guilty person?" Answer: Because you are stronger, and you are the one

listening to God. (See *Lord, Change Me*, by Evelyn Christensen, 2008.)

- However, as the spiritually growing mate, you should not have an attitude of superiority or an attitude of "I am better than you" because your spouse probably knows you are closer to the Lord.

- You should not point out the lack of spiritual growth in your mate, nor share with the wrong attitude how much God is doing for you. Be truthful and share God's goodness, but share in love. This one can be sensitive and needs lots of prayer.

- Listen, talk, encourage, and build up the weaker mate with admiration and do not put him or her down with disdain.

- When past failures and problems are prominent, couples tend to see the future as negative and with no hope of solving the problems. The comments are usually, "It will never change!" God is still in the miracle-working business. With God's help, many marriages have seen His miracle power change things.

2. Ask God for a Vision of Hope for the Future – In other words, begin to do the following:

- Seek a positive, changed future.

- Speak positive and encouraging words for both of you on future ideas.

- You cannot speak these as truths until you change your inner person, with God's help, into positive thinking. Ask God to provide positive thoughts. Proverbs 23:7a states, "For as he thinks in his heart, so is he" (NKJV). Be consistent with your thought patterns. Do not say, "He refuses to read the Bible!" or "She always refuses to listen!" Instead, you might say, "When we read the Bible ..."

Appendix B: Problems or Causes for Divorce or Separation

Over a period of time, one or two factors or problems in a marriage, if not corrected, may lead to thoughts of divorce or to an actual divorce. The following is a list of situations that can develop into huge problems if they are not addressed. With God's help, these situations can be solved. The Lord desires your marriage to work—even more than you do—because marriage is a picture of Christ and the Church. However, it will take application of biblical principles, dependence on the Lord, and persistent daily work to overcome these hindrances and create a strong marriage. Sometimes, one person can work to overcome these issues, but most likely, it will take work on the part of both the husband and the wife.

1. SINS: Sins manifest when either spouse is unfaithful, commits adultery, or indulges in drugs, alcohol, or pornography.

2. METHODS: Differences in methods of doing things can cause problems. Either spouse may say, "We need to do this my way!" or "No, my way is better!"

3. ISOLATION/MOODINESS: When couples withdraw over unsolved problems, one or both may become isolated or moody until they get their way.

4. DECISIONS: Problems can occur when one spouse makes all the minor and major decisions through bullying, manipulation, expressed hurts, or domineering attitudes. Problems can also occur when one spouse carries all the workload and has to make all the decisions.

5. FINANCES: Couples may have differences regarding how to spend money or how to handle the family finances.
   - Some may think the type of furniture to buy or whether to have a big, expensive house is the most important financial decision.
   - Some may want cars, trucks, boats, and fishing equipment.
   - Some may want expensive clothes, jewelry, and shoes.

6. RULES/CHILDREN: Problems can occur when there is disagreement over how to raise children, how to punish them for wrong actions, or what duties and responsibilities each child should have and at what age. Spouses may say,

"My parents did it this way" or "Well, I think we should do it this way!"

7. LACK OF COMMUNICATION SKILLS: Miscommunication can occur when one spouse talks and the other one leaves the room without communicating. If one spouse screams, yells, uses a harsh voice, or expresses accusations, the other spouse may respond with anger, hurt, offensive or defensive language, and may say something he or she later regrets.

8. NO MUTUAL INTERESTS: When one spouse wants to go fishing, boating, or surfing, but the other spouse cannot stand any of these activities, or when one spouse loves to watch sports on television while the other spouse prefers antique shopping, there may be a lack of mutual interests in the marriage.

9. DIFFERENCES IN WORK HABITS or WORK ETHICS: One spouse might be lazy, not want to do any chores or work for a living, or only wants to do enough to get by. The other spouse may be a workaholic and works all the time, but does not set aside any time for fun in his or her marriage. A spouse might stay late at work, and so it seems to the other spouse that the office is more important than home life.

10. DIFFERENCES IN VALUES: One spouse might be a stoic law keeper with many rules, while the other spouse is flexible or lax in values. This couple does not find compromise on a good values system. It might be that neither has good value principles, or perhaps one spouse may have been brought up in a good home, while the other spouse did not live in a good home with set moral values.

11. FAILURES: One spouse might have a lack of mercy and forgiveness when the other spouse fails or has a weakness. The spouse who is strong might express a superior or proud attitude instead of showing humility or helping the weaker spouse.

12. LACK OF LOVE EXPRESSIONS: One or both spouses may lack the ability to express manifested love actions due to childhood issues. Love is action: words, deeds, thoughtful communications, and trips, for example.

13. INTIMATE TIME: A lack of romance or time with each other for intimacy may occur when one or both spouses are too busy with other things or too tired and forget their mates.

14. LACK OF DISCIPLINED PRAYER LIFE: One or both spouses may omit prayer time with the Lord due to schedules, busyness, or a lack of priority for prayer.

15. NO ONENESS IN MARRIAGE: When spouses cannot agree on anything, they may drift apart slowly due to jobs, over-commitment, busyness, or a lack of mutual interests or other things.

16. OVERDEPENDENCE ON PARENTS: One spouse may refuse to let go of time and activities with his or her parents and, thus, cause the other spouse to neglect his or her parents. The couple may be dependent upon their parents for financial help, with the parents bailing them out of problems, which keeps the couple from growing up and maturing.

17. DIFFERENCES IN PERSONALITIES AND BACKGROUNDS: Some couples let their differences in personalities control their environment. Some let their backgrounds influence their behaviors and do not try to understand each other.

18. PAST CHILDHOOD INJURIES DUE TO ABUSE OF ALL TYPES – PHYSICAL, MENTAL, EMOTIONAL: Some spouses may have been abused as children and were not able to tell anyone; thus, they may need some counseling for healing in their adult life or marriage.

19. PHYSICAL OR EMOTIONAL INJURIES: Post-traumatic stress disorder (PTSD) or other types of injuries may cause undue emotional instabilities or problems. Mental or

emotional trauma and problems not solved before or during a marriage may cause problems in the marriage.

20. COUPLES MAY HAVE EXTREME MATURITY LEVELS: Sometimes a person may not develop into maturity because he or she has had his or her "own way" most or all of the time because the person was the baby of the family, or the person "threw fits" and was not corrected while growing up. One spouse may be a "party pal," and the other spouse may be an educated, reserved personality.

Consider these factors, and perhaps other factors, and depend on the Lord to show you how to apply biblical principles to overcome them. Correct these issues now to avoid problems later. With God's help, these situations can be solved. Work with God and with each other to overcome any hindrances that presents threats to your marriage, and rely on the truth of God's Word to build a godly marriage together.

"Rick and Yvonneke Beelby have applied the Bible principles discussed in this book and have enjoyed a godly marriage for 52 years."

Resources

Berry, M. (2019). *Covered by grace.* Xlibris.

Bridges, J. (2012). *Who am I? Identity in Christ.* Cruciform Press.

Chapman, G. (2015). *The five love languages: The secret to love that lasts* (reprint ed.). Northfield Publishing.

Childs, G. (1995). *Understand your temperament! A guide to the four temperaments: Choleric, Sanguine, Phlegmatic, and Melancholic.* Rudolf Steiner Press.

Christenson, E. (2008). *Lord, change me.* Evelyn Christenson Ministry.

Constantino, F. (1985). *More than a miracle: The ministry of aftercare.* PTL Enterprises.

Elevation Church. (2016, August 15). *The prison of offense | The other half | Pastor Steven Furtick* [Video]. YouTube. https://www.youtube.com/watch?v=RwXqcOMw0ng

Evans, J. (2019). *Marriage on the Rock: The comprehensive guide to a solid, healthy and lasting marriage* (rev. & exp. ed.). XO Publishing.

Graham, B. (2006). *Hope for each day: Words of wisdom and faith*. Thomas Nelson.

Hagee Ministries. (2024, March 14). *Pastor Matt Hagee – "The broken borders of marriage"* [Video]. YouTube. https://www.youtube.com/watch?v=dXARBIC5URU

LaHaye, T. (1994). *Spirit-controlled temperament: The best-selling classic on who you are and who you can become*. Tyndale House.

Littauer, F. (2000). *Personality plus: How to understand others by understanding yourself*. Fleming H. Revell.

Luna, T. (2020, March 8). *The body language myth*. Psychology Today. https://www.psychologytoday.com/us/blog/surprise/202003/the-body-language-myth

Shebley, C. (2018). *House construction blueprints* [Photograph]. Flickr. https://www.flickr.com/photos/25636851@N03/41912412672 [House Construction Blueprints by ShebleyCL is licensed under CC BY 2.0.]

Soldier of God – Joyce Meyer. (2022, May 26). *Joyce Meyer – Stop feeding the flesh and this is why | Enjoying everyday life*

[Video]. YouTube.
https://www.youtube.com/watch?v=nlUaocaxXVA

Teague, P. (2020). *Identity: 21 days to the real you.* CreateSpace.

The Bible – Recovery Version. (n.d.). *Section one: A synopsis of the book of Revelation.* Living Stream Ministry.
https://bibleread.online/all-books-by-Watchman-Nee-and-Witness-Lee/book-collected-works-of-watchman-nee-the-set-1-vol-03-the-christian-1-Watchman-Nee-read-online/9/

Van Alstine, E. (2016). *Automatic influence: New power for change in work and life.* Stone Lounge Press.

Wheat, E. (1983). *How to save your marriage alone.* Zondervan.

Wheat, E., & Perkins, G. O. (2001). *Staying in love for a lifetime.* BBS Publishing.

Wright, H. N. (2012). *Communication: Key to Your Marriage* (rev. & upd. ed.). Bethany House.

www.ingramcontent.com/pod-product-compliance
Lightning Source LLC
Chambersburg PA
CBHW071727120626
46550CB00002B/411